SEERS IN THE KINGDOM

(THEIR STORIES)

BY
RAMON SANTOS

Copyright © 2013 Ramon Santos
ISBN: 1493782487
ISBN 13: 9781493782482

All rights reserved. This book is protected by the copyright laws of the United States of America. This book may not be copied or reprinted for commercial gain or profit. The use of short quotations or occasional page copying for personal or group study is permitted. Permission will be granted upon request. Unless otherwise identified, Scripture quotations are from the HOLY BIBLE, ENGLISH STANDARD VERSION© 2001 by Crossway Bibles, a publishing ministry of Good News Publishers. Used by permission. All rights reserved. Scripture quotations marked (NIV) are taken from the HOLY BIBLE, NEW INTERNATIONAL VERSION®. Copyright © 1973, 1978, 1984 by International Bible Society. Used by permission of Zondervan. All rights reserved. Scripture quotations marked (NASB) are taken from the HOLY BIBLE, THE NEW AMERICAN STANDARD BIBLE®. Copyright © 1960, 1962, 1963, 1968, 1971, 1972, 1973, 1975, 1977, 1995 by The Lockman Foundation, La Habra, CA. All rights reserved. Used by permission. (www.Lockman.org). Scripture quotations marked "MSG" are taken from The Message. Copyright 1993, 1994, 1994, 1996, 2000, 2001, 2002. Used by permission of NavPress Publishing Group, www.navpress.com. Scripture quotations marked (ASV) are taken from the AMERICAN STANDARD VERSION BIBLE. Public Domain.

TABLE OF CONTENTS

Preface · *ix*
Introduction · *xiii*
Chapter 1 Design · 1
Chapter 2 The Sierras · 19
Chapter 3 A Jacob Heart · 31
Chapter 4 Noble Saints of Ancient Times · · · · · · · · · · · · 41
Chapter 5 Embracing Design and Star of Grace · · · · · · · · 57
Chapter 6 Feelers, Knowers and Salvation · · · · · · · · · · · · 75
Chapter 7 William's Story, South Africa · · · · · · · · · · · · · 85
Chapter 8 God Humor · 99
Chapter 9 India and the Mark West Story · · · · · · · · · · · 107
Closing · *117*
Other quotes by Teddy Roosevelt · · · · · · · · · · · · · · · · · *119*
Appendix · *121*
About the Author · *125*
Other Books by Ramon Santos · · · · · · · · · · · · · · · · · *127*

THE CHALLENGE

For those of you who are gifted as diviners, mystic readers or psychics, or those who rely on science without a knowledge of God, I invite you to take the journey of Truth, and come to know Jesus Christ.

May He reveal His Love to you as only He can.

Take the challenge. You have nothing to lose, but so much to gain!

VENERATES AND ACKNOWLEDGEMENTS

FIRST, I say thank you to my wife Lorrie. You are my truest friend, lover and companion. You have held my hand and I yours in times of joy, laughter, in destitution, in wealth and in victory. I also bow down with thanks to my children Jacob, Joshua, Josiah and new to our family, Cara, our daughter in law, for the things they teach me.

To my family: I would especially like to acknowledge Grandfather Clement Stitt, Grandmother Fannie Witherspoon, Robinette Witherspoon, Adolph Witherspoon, Emanuel and Mary Witherspoon, Aunt Mary and Uncle Charlie Battle, all my cousins, and William (Bill) Kienzel. To my parents Raymond and Audrey Santos: thank you for loving us pushing us to be better and to go after our dreams. You taught me, to go after what you want. Thanks to my sisters and their husbands, Anita and Mitch Celaya III and Tracy and Bob Vezer, who continue to inspire me. To my in-laws, Chris and George Roberts-Hague I just want to say thank you for standing by us and encouraging us to grow in each other and in Christ. You are a testimony of God love. To Aunt Dorothy Roberts, who in her nineties, has welcomed, encouraged and spoken of God's grace continually, encouraging me in His journeys.

To those I call or have called mentors in times past, those who have helped to keep me on track: It is each one of you that have touched my life in ways that allowed me to grow and to share what has been given me. I say thank you to Dan McCollam, Randy Clark, John Eldridge, John and Carol Arnott, *Toronto Airport Christian Fellowship Teams and Catch the Fire,* David Crone, *The Mission Teams,* Cleddie Keith, Ivan Tate, Bob Jones, Bill and Beni Johnson, Kris Vallotton, *Bethel Church Teams,* Rick Joyner, *The Morningstar Teams,* Wayne and Diane LaCosse for believing in me. Those imparting a piece of legacy into me, for the times we traveled together.

There are many other encouragers and intercessors I have missed. I say thank you to you; you know who you are. Never stop encouraging. There are many others who need what you have, as I did.

And finally, many thanks to the team that helped me in putting together the manuscripts of *Seers in the Kingdom* (*Their Stories*) and *Chronicles of a Seer.* I could not have done it without you: Carol C., Regina McCollam and my daughter-in-law, Cara Santos.

P.S. I ask the Angelic hosts of heaven with the Holy Spirit to continue moving and releasing in you and through you, the will of God and the desires of your heart. I pray this in Jesus' name. Amen.

PREFACE

I believe the reason the Holy Spirit searches deep within the hearts of men and women is not only to know our real intentions, but to know how much authority and power can be released through us. The power and authority available to us is vital to our success as those born to rule and take dominion over the earth.

No matter where we go or what we do, the battles we fight will always be against principalities, cosmic powers, the present darkness, spiritual forces, and the authorities of evil.[2] These evil spirits have started many wars, based in pride and prejudice, throughout history. It will take power and authority, released through the lives of obedient, transformed hearts, to vanquish these powers of darkness on Earth. As we are exercised by the Holy Spirit to learn how to handle this power and authority, our hearts are transformed and we actually grow into our prophetic gift, becoming more able to receive insight, knowledge and understanding from God. We can then release it, with power and authority, to the world around us.

---

2 Ephesians 6:11-12.

In *Seers in the Kingdom*, this *ro'eh*[3] shares the stories of authority and power given to individuals in their lives.

These people fall into two different categories that we will call "seers" and "hearers." The word "prophet" covers both, as it describes one who receives from God.

There is a wisdom I have found: proficient seers begin to carry, over time, the ability to say what will manifest in the present and the future, using a past reference as a launching point. They can also tell what will transpire if certain conditions are or are not fulfilled. They are teachers of spirit knowledge that transcends time, bringing clarity, often communicating with an intensity that may seem a bit overboard. An example of this would be the story of General William (Billy) Mitchell of the United States Air Force giving detailed events of the bombing of Pearl Harbor years before it even happened.[4] I'm sure at the time of his delivery, people thought he was a bit crazy.

The seers and hearers have great potential as they work together as the prophetic voice, releasing the Word of God from Heaven's realm. Seers and hearers in the Spirit are very unique, with differing strengths and weaknesses, comparable to people defined as "nearsighted" and "farsighted". Each hearer and seer will also be unique within their category. For example, while people with the ability to hear (in the natural) all receive and interpret sound, some may hear unique tones, allowing them to compose music, while others have relative pitch, or tone deafness even. Similarly, each prophet will be unique and varied in his or her ability to see and hear and then communicate their message.

---

3 The Hebrew term *ro'eh* refers more to Old Testament prophets as described in 1 Samuel 9:9 and 2 Chronicles 29:25.

4 Santos, Ramon. *Chronicles of a Seer*, Chapter 1.

The delivery of the seer revelation brings the gifting through the transparency of emotion in its release within a group setting or to an individual. Most seers have a way of moving passionately and wholeheartedly, while a hearer's delivery may seem more subdued because of the depth of the revelation he received. Neither is superior to the other; a person without much empathy may be moved by words of knowledge from a hearer over the intricate, revelatory depth of a seer. Someone more emotionally driven may have the opposite experience. The two, working together in the unity of the Spirit, however, can project their message of the Kingdom much further than they ever could functioning as a single unit. This is the benefit of teams and I believe is one of the reasons why the Jesus sent the Apostles out in pairs.

The term "seer" in modern times is thought of more in relation to prophetic dreams and visions.

> *"And in the last days it shall be," God declares, "that I will pour out my Spirit on all flesh, and your sons and your daughters shall prophesy, and your young men shall see visions, and your old men shall dream dreams; even on my male servants and female servants in those days I will pour out my Spirit, and they shall prophesy. And I will show wonders in the heavens above and signs on the earth below"* (Acts 2:17-19).

I encourage you to put on your armor, move forward with seers and hearers and actively participate in love as the Kingdom of Heaven is taken by force.[5]

Jesus clearly defined our mandate:

---

5 Matthew 11:12, and 1 John.

I only do what I see the Father doing (John 5:19).

This is one of many ways Jesus Himself communicated as a seer and hearer throughout the New Testament: He established on earth what He heard and saw His Father doing.

To study more about "seers" and "hearers," I recommend that you search the Scriptures. Begin in Genesis, as the Old Testament stories detail the way prophecy was used. Then read the New Testament (I prefer the English Standard Version, by the way) where we see vivid examples of how we, as children of the Most High, receive the love of the Father. Sadly, many teach and still live out of the Old Testament ways with a mindset of a slave-to-master relationship to God. Jesus, however, clearly invited us into a deeper, more intimate relationship He shared with His Father by calling us His friends. From this favored position we deliver His message to the world.

I started my own personal biblical study on this subject with the New King James version paralleled to ESV. I especially love Jesus' words, highlighted in red, which I have found makes His message clearer and easier to understand.

Jesus' blood sealed a covenant of inheritance in the Fathers love for His children. This is our message to the world and the testimonials recorded in *Seers in the Kingdom*.

INTRODUCTION

A SEER IS ONE who has the ability to traverse into different dimensions as a spectator in the realms of time and space. This is known as Euclidean space perception. Though you can do nothing but passively view revelation of the past, present and future in this state, the seer is found in paradox; while they are spectators in their viewing, they can actually do something and effect change with what they've seen. Over time, a seer begins to understand the releasing of their knowledge and how it can and does change circumstances for the betterment of oneself and others to edify the world we live in. It also brings wisdom for the moment or seasons to come.

Regardless of their revelation and leading, seers and hearers all have choices to make. This is especially true in times of the common, inconvenient afflictions of life. In my life, it has been my wife, Lorrie, and her wisdom that has frequently helped me to understand the correct course of action to take. Walking in the Spirit and being directed by prophetic revelation is like having one's life-course adjusted to a destination yet to be revealed. Then, along the way, having beacons lit for points of reference on the journey. Prophetic wisdom, messages or insight are like those beacons. And yet, while we may see a way lit before us, we still have to choose what course we will take. Here is something I once heard; it is worth remembering:

> *When you go before a judge you cannot say, "He told me to do it," or "It was not convenient at the time." Our choices are in our keeping alone, when we stand before God or man.*

There are answers to our questions as we try to make decisions, if we are willing to see or hear what is spoken and then release it. Let me emphasize this: when you see or hear a revelation, do not push aside what is revealed. Check it and double check it, always using love as the key. Remember the Golden Rule: "Whatever you wish that others would do to you, do also to them (Matthew 7:12)."

The supernatural is a combination of science, miracles and wonders that are all signs of God's finger touching us. Choices are given to us to make this a better world for all nations, because we are all His children. God loves us, and wants the best for us. He gives us the capacity to join with Him, releasing His best for the world through our choices. To me, our choices are one avenue we can take to fulfill the commandments in Matthew 22:37-40. I have lived by these verses since my youth. They have never steered me wrong: *"Love the Lord your God with all your heart, soul and mind"*, and secondly, *"Love your neighbor as yourself."* If you make these two things your focus, base all of your choices around them, everything else will fall into place.

TERMS

Jim Goll uses two words to define certain revelations. In his book, *The Seer*,[7] Goll uses the word *visual* to describe the actual sight, dream or vision a person or persons has into another dimension. He uses the word *actual* to describe the manifest powers that come from the visual contents being released. This is the power of the heavenly presence God being released.

I prefer to use the word "ethereal" instead of *actual* which to me refers to the heavenly or celestial regions beyond the earth. I will be using both words to describe events in this book. There is authority granted to us when we carry and release the presence of God, because His presence brings power. It is with this presence that many unexplainable, documented signs and wonders happen today.[8]

What good is authority without power to back it up? It is authority stamped with power that brings the ethereal into play. For examples of this, consider Daniel. In Daniel chapter eight, we see Daniel interceding for his people. In this time, he received revelation about things to come. In the presence of the arch angel, Gabriel, Daniel lost all strength and fell on his face. He experienced *theurgy*: the working of a divine or supernatural being in human affairs. In these encounters, we often experience an interaction with power. You see, when we interact with spiritual beings, especially with the Lord, we are interacting with the ethereal, the spiritual, the realm

---

7 Goll, Jim. *The Seer*, Destiny Image Publications.

8 John 14:12.

that we cannot touch with our natural hands. But, power is both ethereal and natural and bridges the gap between these realms.

Remember, there are two main sources that we can receive prophetic information from: a heavenly, good source or an unheavenly virus-like demonic source. There is power and authority in both sources. But, it is God's authority and power that created all things; His is the Supreme Power, and it is given to His children.

> *Everything was created through him; nothing—not one thing!—came into being without him* (John 1:3, MSG).

> *And the Word became flesh and dwelt among us, and we have seen His glory, glory as of the only Son from the Father, full of grace and truth* (John 1:14).

CHAPTER 1

DESIGN

IN SOCIETY THERE ARE critical needs that all individuals have. These include needs such as water, food, clothing, shelter; health-related issues, relationships, followed by growth in knowledge to maintain and improve these conditions, along with one's desires. In time, experience leads to knowledge. Knowledge releases greater understanding on the importance of these needs. The ability to eat and nourish oneself and family, the ability to keep out disease, sickness, and corruption are all critical needs for individuals as well as communities. These needs are critical places to begin as you release the Kingdom.

We are designed with the same basic needs. However we are not all designed with the same gift mixes, strengths, weaknesses, desires or preferences. One is not inferior to the other, just different. This is very important to realize as we are ministering the Kingdom. While there are common needs to focus on, how we will minister to them will change based on our God-given design.

I want to share this story of one who describes his experience of seeing, in the form of a short story. Though his gift leads him to help meet the needs of those around him, he is not always sure what to do with it. He, like all of us, needs to become familiar with his own personal design.

Mariel Vanessa Tolocker by Joshua

When I was a six-year old child, I learned very quickly that most others cannot see the things I see. At first, when I mentioned the disgusting things hovering around many, my parents assumed that I had "imaginary friends" or that I simply had a greater preference for imagining things around me than other children. I believe it's when I described, in detail, a demon hovering around my father and picking at a spot where he had been injured that he got a little freaked out. He simply told me that I needed to stop playing pretend and that I should pay more attention to the real world. That was right before he went into his room for a "lay down" because his shoulder was acting up and causing him pain. As he entered his room, I remember seeing that unclean 'thing' paying an inordinate amount of attention to me. It didn't stop what it was doing.

After that time, those creatures seemed to swarm around my house. Looking for any way to get in, or attach themselves to those around me who were invited in. Day or night, there was no member of my family who didn't have one of those things attached to them, nor did they ever stop leering at me whenever I was in sight. No matter how much I told my parents about the creatures, or tried to get them to throw the things off, they never seemed to believe me. It was as though they closed themselves off to me and considered whispers from these things that I couldn't hear.

Two weeks after the things started swarming my home, my parents paid a psychologist to come and visit me, after failing to convince me to go see him. Whatever had happened to him in the past, he looked positively frightening now. The man had three demons on him. There were two on his shoulders and one hanging on to his right arm; moreover his head looked like it had been cracked open and his brain exposed. I didn't say a word to him; he looked so much like a doll as he spoke to me.

It was like the whispers from one told him what he should say, the second one actually reached through that crack into his mind so that he spoke it, and the third directed his course of action in what he wrote. At the end of the words spoken between my parents and him, he finished writing a prescription of medicine. When he looked at it, he seemed surprised for a few seconds up until one whispered something more and the other played with his head.

In the end, he simply gave my mother the prescription of medicine, and reached into his doctor's bag, pulling out a bottle of the prescription pills. While handing her both the bottle and his bill, the demon hanging on his arm reach over to the pill bottle touching it and filling it with something dark and unclean. No one else noticed.

After he left, when my mother tried to have me take the medicine at the appropriate time, I refused. Of course, it wasn't anywhere near as easy as that; I was disciplined with anything from spankings to being grounded unless I took the pills. When my mother looked to be about at the end of her rope, she tried to cook the pills into my plate of food in various ways. After the third attempt, where I ate everything but the dirtied food in question, she seemed to realize something and looked at me with a speculative gaze. For the first time that I could remember since mentioning the creatures, she seemed to be dismissing whatever was being whispered to her.

She started getting into arguments with Papa about me, and things seemed to come to a head a few days later. Papa finally took me into his lap and tried to force the pill down my throat. I bit him instead, dropping out of his lap and getting behind Mother. He seemed to be in shock for a while, as I had never bitten him before in my life. Finally, he simply shook his head and told Mother to do as she liked. He wouldn't get involved.

It was a month afterwards that my parents, primarily my mother, called a Catholic priest over and asked him to exorcise any demons out of me that he could. While I didn't feel any different or see anything come out of me, all the demons that had been hanging around up until this point departed at the command to leave in the name of "Jesus Christ of Nazareth." I asked the man what it took to be able to invoke that Name and he responded that it only took the desire to serve Jesus and have faith. No works could make one worthy, and no amount of religious fervor could make it a natural ability. He left me a simple wooden cross on a string and I haven't seen him since.

Time passed. I prayed to Jesus for protection over myself and my family. The demons returned, however, even though I prayed for them to be sent elsewhere. I did not tell my family what I saw. Sometimes the creatures managed to cling to those who came in; other times they were cast out. The rest of my family seemed to think that my sight of things unnatural was caused by a demon and that my new-found religion kept it from returning. I didn't say anything to the contrary, though once in a while, my mother and father would look at me speculatively.

When I turned nine, my great aunt Sarah was attacked by a robber and everyone had come to the hospital to check on her. She was supposed to be in traction for two months with several broken bones. I, being the youngest, had to wait outside the room until everyone else paid their respects. It was then that I learned, from observation, just how dangerous hospitals could be for those who have no faith in God, nor any to pray for them. Demons are constantly flitting around the place—especially on a full moon night—doing everything in their power to wound people, distract doctors, cause them to forget a medical procedure, reopen old wounds, and cause complications to arise with treatments. Now, at the time, I wasn't aware of the full scope of the activities of these demons.

Many times, I saw a dirty creature speed by and stop to dig at everyone in the room, once or twice it managed to hit something soft but it didn't seem to find anything to hold on to. A few times, my aunt's doctor walked by with the same creature on his shoulder, whispering something to him. After he walked by it would return, usually to try and chip at the spot it attacked before. Once, the doctor seemed about ready to stop and talk to us, despite the whisper that he heard, only to be paged to attend to another patient that had sudden complications.

About the only good thing that stood out in this visit was that in several rooms the creatures seemed to be prevented entry somehow, and in at least three that I saw, there was a person that just looked clean and wholesome standing guard over a patient. One guardian had a sword that seemed to shine with an inner light that he held ready. I could not look at it directly and gauge its shape. Another guardian had a shafted weapon that seemed to shift from being a spear one moment and then change to various weapons as I continued watching.

It was the third room that made my jaw drop. There were four figures standing guard over a heavily-wounded individual whose face I could not see. The first three seemed to be arranged in a circle around his bed facing outward, a weapon of some kind in hand. The fourth seemed to hover over the bed; he was semi-transparent as though he wasn't fully there.

His attention seemed to be locked onto the hospital itself. I think he saw me, but I'm not sure because he seemed to be making gestures and effecting things I could not see. At least once I saw a creature come into the room he resided in, and before it even reached halfway to the bed with the other guardians, it disappeared by means of some word he spoke. I could not see where it went. He was the only one of the figures that was unarmed. Another time, the doctor was about to pass by the room, but he said something and pointed. The thing whispering in his ear halted, disappearing as the doctor took notice and attended to the patient in the room, unaware of the others in the room or the fact that he was about to pass them by.

I returned home with my family and we went on with our lives, praying for my aunt in the process. Eventually, after several close calls, our aunt came to live with us. While she got better, I noticed that the same creature that had been tormenting her, and those in the hospital, popped up from time to time, trying to find some place to lay a hold of and dig in. I haven't stopped praying for her since.

Ever since that time, I have been wary of most hospitals. Whenever the conversation turns towards such a thing, I remind those I'm speaking to that until full health has returned to them, the enemy will seek to drag them back to a place where they may be wounded regularly with ease.

THE UNSEEN NECESSITIES

Prophetic people see and hear many of the needs that surround individuals and communities that are not visual in the natural. When the opportunity presents itself, they step forward to take on the condition, whether it is something that needs to be done in the natural or in the unseen realms. The seer in this story was stepping in to bring protection in the form of intercession. Intercession is released in many layers and may affect the present, past, or a time to come. However it may be revealed, it will come with knowledge, wisdom, authority and power to handle what is transpiring.

There are times seers are not sure of what they perceive or how they should respond. They may back away from the whole ordeal. Unfortunately, this impotence leads to cycles of re-occurring experiences that only end when the seer will respond appropriately to what he has seen. Remember: God wants change for the better. These seers must act to release what God has intended for the circumstance. I have seen cases where the seer does not step up, does not act in the authority he has, and similar events will repeat again and again until this passivity is no longer an option. That seer or hearer steps forward to stop the cycle by the means revealed to him as he receives knowledge and acts as an intercessor.

This is one of the ways seers learn that they can make the difference. For them, it is not about running for help, but standing in the gap to make the difference. There are times the unclean spirits know a seer's fear and continue to torment right in front of him or her until the seer learns what to do, which brings us back to needs.

The law of supply and demand creates a flow in which needs are met. We have needs that put a demand on that which supplies them. When we have what we need, the pressure to get more diminishes. However, there are needs that can only be met by God. It is said and proven that faith and works cannot be done apart; we cannot do works to meet our needs without faith to empower our efforts, filling them with power and authority. Without faith, all of our efforts are hollow, at best.

One of our greatest needs is to know ourselves, to know what to do with ourselves. We need to learn to recognize what we need as individuals and to begin changing the world, starting inside of ourselves.

In the natural, we as societies build infrastructure for communities that are growing to support their demands for a healthy life. If one or more of our core needs are not meet over time, we begin to seek—or create—other avenues to fill them. We begin to create infrastructures in our own little worlds in an attempt to satisfy our needs through misguided means. But trying to control our environments or control others will not work. In his song, "Man in the Mirror," Michael Jackson, the King of

Pop, says if you want to make a change, you should look in the mirror and start there: start with you. Since each and every day is a challenge, we strive to improve our lives and lives of others. This may start with the desire to improve simple economics, or diversify society but what we start with good intentions might have the wrong values. And while we cannot always judge right from wrong, we are called to preserve the Earth with truth (Matthew 5:13). If asked, we are called to give a loving solution with Truth.

Not everyone will accept truth, and this hurts at times. I have personally lost friends because we had different sets of values. I couldn't violate my standards, and they wouldn't give up the convenience of being able to do whatever they wanted, so we parted ways.

People often try to validate their poor value systems by making excuses. This is convenient. It means that they don't have to change. I've heard excuses like, "It's just in their makeup." It's not in their makeup. It is not how they were designed. Their choices made them into who they are today. Many of these choices they've made out of places of pain. They change their values and standards, following other misguided people, and this leaves an opening for unclean principalities mixing verisimilitude[10] with Truth.

Many people have been taught correctly. They know Truth, but justify and even hide negative changes, particularly changes in their value systems. They do so as to not embarrass themselves, their family or friends. We all face this, or similar circumstances,

---

10   Appearance of Truth.

in our lives at one time or another. This form of trepidation still allows a form of gratification as they come into agreement in some way. Fear and a sense of freedom begin to coexist in this lifestyle. These people make a change in their morality but mask it with the false appearance of Truth. However, it is not our appearance that shows who we are. It is our decisions that define who we are and where we are going. Our choices, not our neatly designed exteriors, will determine the legacy or excess we can leave behind as an inheritance.

When you stand before God, it will be you alone with Christ, answering for the decisions you made throughout life. I say, do not judge; I have my own stones to lie down, as we all do. This, however, does not mean I have to come into agreement with immorality, wickedness, deceit, or coveting, to name a few of those unclean principalities. It says in the Bible to leave all judgments in God's hands. It is the Holy Spirit that searches the intents and the heart, and I believe that in this position, God discerns with love and grace. With the measure we use He will use.[11]

For more on this subject, read *Decisions that Define Us*, by David Crone. It will take you into another realm of understanding regarding the power of your decisions.[13]

As for me and my defining decisions, I speak, "As for me and my house, with my children, we serve the Lord our God, in Jesus name."

---

11 Matthew 7:2, Mark 4:24, Luke 6:28.
13 Crone, David. *Decisions that Define Us.* Available on Amazon.com.

STEADFAST

Even if you do not believe in God, the Golden Rule still applies. I am called to accept you with love, as a person, not any misguided values or false appearances of Truth.[15] Every human being has the right to respect, to kindness and to love. That is what the Golden Rule is all about. We all have desires, whatever they may be, good or bad. At times, our desires conflict with our values- what we should and should not do- but the Golden Rule stands the test of time; love stands the test of time. It's God's love that enables us to love one another. We are made in His image, whether we know Him or not! Our morals do not improve us. They are limited, being a verisimilitude,[16] but our love for one another, for us to use and share, is what will change life as we know it.

Humanity cannot possibly endure and conquer all life challenges without Jesus Christ. We are in a constant pursuit for the Source of every resource- everything we'll ever need. Whether you believe in God or not, stop and think about it. Why do scientists search for adaptations, acceleration within life? Why do communities focus on improvement to gain necessities, and for the betterment of mankind? It is because there is more than what we have. God has it. And our resources and abilities, including engineering, humanitarian work and science are to be a part of mankind's growth along with a relationship in Jesus Christ.

Our progress is not based in works. I have done many things, walking in the gifts with authority and power given to me through

---

15 Matthew 7:12, 22:37.

16 Appearance of Truth.

Jesus. Success is in seeking a deeper relationship with the Trinity (the Father, the Son, the Holy Spirit) as they are One and the same, as I am in Christ. They are in me and I in them as the Holy Spirit is in and around us the power of the Godhead.[18] And though Christ separated from the Father for our redemption at one time, the splendor of glory was given back to Christ at His resurrection as He became Spirit and Flesh again. That is the glory that He has now given to us!

In John 17:5, Jesus asked:

> *Father, glorify me in your own presence with the glory that I had with you before the world existed.*

A simple understanding of the Trinity can be found by reading theses verses: Genesis 1, John 1:1-3, 14.

It was the following words spoken in Matthew that brought new meaning to the word "relationship" to many in Christ. It clearly illustrates that our relationship with Him is not based on our works. There is much more. Remember works are needed with faith and faith with works. But they are not one and the same.

> *On that day many will say to me, "Lord, Lord, did we not prophesy in your name, and cast out demons in your name, and do many mighty works in your name?" And then will I declare to them, "I never knew you; depart from me, you workers of lawlessness"* (Matthew 7:22-23).

---

18 John 14:17, 17:21.

Our forefathers left their homelands to establish America, because this aspect of relationship with God, a personal relationship, was not available to them under the religious system of the day. Because of this, coupled with the hope of a better life, they left everything behind in search of freedom to pursue the needs of their hearts and lives. In the infrastructure of life some have steered away from the love, truth, joy and peace that were created to be a part of life journeys from the Maker of creation.

There are theories that evolve continually in the creation of the universe from non-believers as scientific advancements and scholar's research have proven them to be false. There was one such educational flaw known as "Darwin's Theory" that have ruined many lives and set many scientists on the wrong path for a century. When that theory was proven false with the tools we have today, we are now removing a wrong foundation. With this revelation many scientists began to have unprecedented breakthroughs in the sciences, especially in the regions of health and the signs of creation pointing to the Creator.

I urge scientists to continue the search for Truth, just as I spent my life searching the Scriptures, transforming my thoughts and ideas. I began to study Biblical history to understand what was happening at the time the Bible accounts were taking place. This allowed me to grasp deeper meaning from the passages, because many of them are not understandable by our modern-day thinking. Some great leaders that I learned from in digging into these roots, were Bill Johnson and John and Carol Arnott. They have given great revelation of the Fathers heart and Love in relationships.[19]

---

19 Bill Johnson, www.iBethel.org. John & Carol Arnott, www.catchthefire.com.

The love of God gives me seeds of growth in life, in the full Gospel of Jesus Christ. It has taught me to love others, hope and persevere, among many other things. Now, if the Gospel is a lie, then that part of my life was not a waste of time. But if my God is real, then everything we are doing- myself, other Christians, scientists and many others—will lead to the Truth of who Jesus Christ is: the Son of the One true God. The lives I touched on the journey, and the lives other seers touch, have proven it has made this a better world for all nationalities.

After in-depth research, scholars are now saying there is Truth in God creating life from speaking words and bringing life. Scholar's research shows through physics that sound resonates and creates. I recommend reading *God Vibrations* by Dan McCollam for a deeper understanding of the creation through spoken words.[20] Here I say the "Big Bang Theory" starts: the speaking of the word of life by God with Christ.

As scientific research develops, so do godly leaders walking in authority and power. They help us receive necessities for our lives. Society's structure is growing, providing positions with many names, to help individuals and communities in their areas of need.

To give you a better understanding of a seer's influence in communities, with the decisions they make and the challenges they face, I recommend reading *Chronicles of a Seer*. Here you will see the Holy Spirit and theurgy at work today, giving a better understanding of unsolved mysteries.

---

20 McCollam, Dan. God Vibrations Study Guide: A Kingdom Perspective on the Power of Sound, 2013. Available on Amazon.com.

In the stories to follow I will be using fictitious names to maintain privacy. Some do not want to be known, others must remain unnamed for their protection. The stories are true, but the time frame may be off. There is a code of conduct those in the stories try to live by. It brings glory and excellence in their life and the lives of others.

CODE OF CONDUCT: 2 PETER 1

1. Supplement: faith with virtue is to add.

2. Faith: act or state of wholeheartedly believing and trusting in.

3. Virtue: moral practice or action (divine law or the highest good), moral excellence, integrity of character, choice of excellence in conduct with excellence.

4. Knowledge: to recognize as being something indicated, the fact or condition of knowing something with a considerable degree of familiarity gained through experience of or contact or association, understanding of some branch of science, art, learning, or other area involving study, research or practice.

5. Self control: resistance exercised over one's own desires or impulses.

6. Steadfastness: firmly established, fixed in a position, marked by unwavering steadiness.

7. Godliness: conforming of one's life to the revealed character and purpose of God, personification, embodiment of God.

8. Brotherly affection: affectionate (governed by passion).

9. Love: the attraction, desire for a person who delight or admiration or elicits tenderness, object of devotion.

   A. Patience and kindness: Does not envy or boast, is not arrogant or rude, it does not insist on its own way, it's not irritable or resentful, it does not rejoice at wrongdoing, but rejoices with the truth.

   B. Love bears all things, believes all things, hopes all things, endures all things.

   C. Love never ends (1Corinthians 13:4-8).

10. Wisdom: effectual mediating principle or personification of God will in creation of the world, accumulated information philosophic or learning.

Remember: When you go before a judge you cannot say, "He told me to do it," or, "It was not convenient at the time." Whether they are CEOs, kings, presidents or prominent officials, our choices are in our keeping alone when we stand before God and man.

CHAPTER 2

THE SIERRAS

THE STEPPING OUT WITH faith and works, or works with faith, that proclaim an unveiling of understanding, infirmities are healed. Creating new roads of travel that expand into highways of learning allows one to walk into the new arenas of life. Think of it this way: when a baby is born this is a new road. Everything changes continually as the baby grows.

Lorrie and I, traveling within the Truckee and Lake Tahoe regions of Northern California, had to pull off to the side of the road, having ethereal visions in day, as the dreams at night brought a greater release of revelation. In one instance, I gazed at the people standing on the Tahoe City Bridge under which a river ran. My eyes open wide in spiritual realms, I watched as the river began rising to great heights. I asked a person standing nearby, "What river is this"? The retort, "The Truckee River."

Later, as I researched the Truckee River, I learned about the Native Americans who had lived along the river, to the source of the water in the Sierra Mountains. This river runs under Lake Tahoe and comes out in Tahoe City. This river has a continuous feed from other mountains that nourish it with freshly melted snow and underground streams. The Truckee River feeds areas starting in California, through the Northern Tahoe area, flowing into the Northern Nevada dry regions, going down and back up, ending at Pyramid Lake, Nevada, providing life-giving water.

Years went by after this, until one day I heard the Lord say to me, "What is your birth name?"

Pausing before answering, "Ramon." The Greek-Spanish meaning of my name is "wise defender, protector of the people." My name had been shortened to Ray. The Lord says to me, "I gave you that name." From then on, I began going by my birth name. From that moment, I started evaluating my life history and how its meaning was spot-on in describing me. I began feeling something was—and is—approaching rapidly, just as Truckee River was rising in spiritual realm.

TRUCKEE & STREET VIBRATIONS

Having bought a Fat-Boy, Harley Davidson motorcycle a month before, I decided to go to Reno, Nevada, for the West Coast Motorcycle rally, "Street Vibrations." Everyone who rides was talking about it being held the last weekend in September every year. The City of Reno shuts down its two main streets to all automobiles and only opens it to motorcycles.

Taking off early Friday afternoon, I got a call shortly afterward from a friend of mine who rides, saying he'd like to meet me in Reno. Lorrie and my friend's wife would meet me us there the next morning. Throwing the packed overnight bag on the Star of David (the name I gave my bike), I headed east on I-80 to Reno on a sunny, ninety degree day.

The traffic got dense on the way in Sacramento, becoming bumper to bumper. As traffic stopped, I split traffic. Then, out of nowhere, it began to pour down rain. It went from a bright, sunny day with a handful of clouds, to a downpour. My stomach was now screaming, "Feed me!" and my bike saying the same thing, so I stopped in the city of Rocklin and grabbed some gas. Seeing a Rocket Café, I headed up the street; it was retro-burger time! I took in a book to pass the time. The next thing I knew, it was 7:30 p.m. As I headed out, the sun was setting in my rearview mirror.

It was a moonless night. Pitch-blackness covered everything and the temperature dropped rapidly. I had ninety-five miles to go. Surprisingly, the darkness brought icy temperatures with snow in September. Who would have thought? Unprepared for this change of weather, I was speeding along with only a t-shirt, a leather vest, and fingerless gloves. Being numb from the freezing temperatures

I was glad to see a sign for Truckee, only twenty-five miles ahead. I began to pray heavily to the Lord while trying to feel my fingers, rotating my hands in turn on the hot engine.

Upon reaching the Old Town of Truckee, a tourist attraction, I pulled in to stop and get warm. The shops were closed; the restaurants and bars so packed, you had to wait outside in the snow for a place to open up. I was told the wait times for a table inside were up to thirty minutes. I was about to give up and get back on the motorcycle, as my body parts had no sensation, when I noticed a lit sign for a restaurant on the second floor above a candy shop. Going up the stairs, shivering, I was greeted and seated at the bar. Getting situated, I finally ordered a slice of hot apple pie with a hot chocolate, thanking God for a place to sit and warm up.

It took a good hour to warm up while reading my book and enjoying those savory bites of apple, caramel and walnuts sailing down my throat. But, I still had thirty-four miles left to Reno. I thanked the waiter for his hospitality and left a good tip. I found my ski gloves in the travel bag as I was looking for my bandana. I also found a coat. It was about 11:00 p.m. when I reached Reno, just as events on the streets where shutting down. Observing motorcycles lining both sides of the streets, this was a first for me. Having found the hotel at the end of the main street strip, I parked the bike in the hotel garage, checked in, and called it a night.

The next morning, I was having breakfast on the third floor of the hotel restaurant as the building vibrated from the roar of the engines below in garage. Heading out on the streets, I found vendors selling items related to motorcycles: parts, clothes and variety of other things that should not be there. In the unseen realms: critters, demons and all kinds of unclean things I have no name for. They were doing what they do best—creating havoc and discontent.

It was great to see some people on some of the corners and other places ministering to those in need. Some were with the Christian Motorcycle Association (CMA) and Bikers for Christ, to name a few. Some even had vendor booths, bring the Word of truth, life and healing to fellow bikers.

This outreach was doing many unseen things in the natural. Some were toiling (making a way). Some were planting; I saw items being put inside of people or rotted things removed. Some were watering. A simple smile caused a body to begin to glow; their hearts, spirits, bodies and minds were expanding and absorbing, as they were being fed. In the natural it looked like simple bottles of water given as a free gift, a hug, or encouraging word. I saw a woman break out in tears from someone handing her money. She was broke, yet had told no one. She knew God had told someone about her need. I was told by another the reason she was broke.

These simple things are needs we all have. Clothing and love are necessities for all. These people were definitely warriors of Christ, some moving in power and authority, many with just the power of love, releasing the Kingdom of God. These ministry groups were making an impact in bringing the lost to the knowledge of Christ Jesus. I watched angelic hosts of Heaven standing guard as some of the unclean spirits were trying to keep the people away. The unclean had attached themselves to the person as God; love drew them in.

Lorrie and the others made it up around 10:00 a.m. We started enjoying the events together. By about 3:00 p.m. everyone was tired and ready to head home. I suggested we stop in Truckee on the way back to get some of that savory apple pie and visit the chocolate candy store below the restaurant.

We reached Old Town Truckee. Parking in front of the establishment and going up the stairs, we noticed a sign that said, "Closed." Going into the candy store, we asked what time the restaurant opens, and the gentleman responded that it had been closed for the last year.

"Hun," I told Lorrie, "I ate there last night!" The store man, shaking his head asked, "What would you like?"

So I left, going to the store next door and got the same response, "It has been closed for a long time." Then realizing it was a wonder! I thanked God for that place of rest knowing now it was truly an encounter with the Kingdom of Heaven.

This you will have to decide for yourself: was it a wonder, or the imagination of one frozen rider on a motorcycle with thirty-four miles still to go?

That pie was fabulous.

KINGDOM ENCOUNTERS

During this time the franchised mortgage business I invested in was at its peak. Lorrie and I felt the need to build a cabin in the mountains of Truckee, feeling led by our visions and Heavenly encounters. We looked for a lot to build on, and found the land through a past client, Jerry, who lived in Truckee. Jerry had decided it was time to sell the land he owned, next door to him. This lot had an underground spring that perks up, creating a creek as it flows down the mountain that never freezes over all year round. It feeds the Truckee River. We bought that lot because of that creek.

We loved that if fed the Truckee River in the natural and it matched our ethereal visions.

Having settled on a Log Homes Company located on east coast, with representatives in Northern California, it was like a dream come true. Except, unfortunately, neither the salesman nor contractor we trusted in fulfilled their commitments and contract obligations so we fired them.

The architect had re-adjusted the structural plans to meet the Town of Truckee standards for approval and we hired new contractors to finish the project. The cost had tripled by time it was finished. The cost to completion went well beyond the original construction loan budget engulfing our entire savings and retirement funds. The six months stretched to three years. The family attorney wanted us to go after the original salesman and contractor. We released it into God's hands. The cabin was given the occupancy certificate December 24, 2006, with a few minor details to be finished after the holidays. It was as beautiful as the visions, dreams and trances would had now transpired in the natural.

People came from all over the country, receiving encounters and healings as God led them, and His finger touched the ministry meetings we had there.

The one occurrence that stands out to me was when I was visiting my friend Hy Kozak, Rabbi of a Messianic Congregation in Reno during their Saturday morning service. I had missed an older woman that showed up looking for me. The Lord told her where to find me. She told the worship leader there that she was to go to the event at our cabin. She stated the Lord told her He would heal her if she went to "Fire on the Mountain" in Truckee.

That night the woman showed up at the cabin. As the team laid hands on her, she started dancing and praising God. The woman was healed of all the infirmities that had plagued her for decades.

Some of the people had no idea why they were coming to Truckee; they just had to come.

TRUCKEE RIVER

There were three major *ethereal* encounters that occurred on the Truckee River during the next three years. First was when the River Rock Christian Fellowship team had gathered, praying and making declarations over the Town of Truckee and other regions of Northern California and Nevada. They were standing in the gap with intercession over historical events against Native Americans and Chinese emigrants. I again saw the river was rising in increasing height, with momentum in the supernatural realm. This was also seen by others in the group.

Month passed by after this event, when the second occurred. This encounter was in the City of Reno, at the River Walk Park which has an island in the middle of the Truckee River. It is connected to banks by bridges, with an amphitheater on the island. There was music and praise going on, led by different worship bands on rotating shifts.

There were people of all ages, denominations and nationalities joining together as one in song, dance and worship. People were playing in the river, bodysurfing, swimming and diving between the boulders over the mini waterfalls created by the rushing water. In surveying the water in natural it was about 10 to 15 feet below the previous level. My eyes sprung into spiritual dimensions as the water was rising in increments. I asked the Lord what it meant, as the river increased in height a few feet, bringing with it intensity as it was now covering some of the boulders. Getting no answer, the event ended.

I returned a year later to same spot, during another worship gathering of the community ministries. This time the heaviness of God's presence was resonating over Reno. It could be felt twenty miles away. The closer we got, the heavier the presence. My sight opened in a mystical way, in time and space, and again, I saw the river was rising, being changed. As I was talking, my speech instantly went into language of tongues.

> *A gift from God for praying in tongues that he gives us for praising him, which leads to wonderful intimacies we enjoy with him* (1Corinthians 14:18, MSG).

We were standing and enjoying the presence. Concurrently, I had to grab ahold of a bridge railing to keep myself from falling into the river from the intense weight of Kingdom presence. I fell to one knee.

Realizing I was hearing the rip-roaring sounds of water rapids rushing through my ears as I was, in essence, seeing myself in the river now. I was feeling the cool water flowing over me, through me, and all around me. Then looking up, I was seeing the water level above my head reaching the top of the river banks ready to overflow into the city.

This was God sharing what He is about to do in the northern regions of both California and Nevada with the outpouring of His Spirit and those willing to partner with Him. He is waiting and releasing into those who are willing step out and carry what is being released to all people in the regions and beyond, to carry the gifts of the Holy Spirit and trust in the Holy Spirit a part of the God head.

I wondered if this was like what Moses felt by stopping to see what the God was doing Exodus 3. Elijah did in Kings 18:41-46 what Christ told the seers of old, Ezekiel (40:2-4), and to Habakkuk, "write down what is revealed…" (2:1-4).

VELOCITY

This Holy Spirit spark of revelation can—and does—ignite many of us, pushing us to finish. This race, win or lose, must be run; it is about finishing. Running the race brings the full Gospel that encompasses authority and power by the strength of love.

Paul said it in 1 Corinthians 1:17.

The only way you lose is by not trying or contending. The song, "Dive," by Steven Curtis Chapman, is one of those catalysts for me as a seer. It moves me to dive into an ethereal encounter.

CHAPTER 3

A JACOB HEART

THERE ARE MANY TRIALS that we inflict upon ourselves, by the choices we make. Some are inflicted on us by others. This event involved me, Lorrie and our oldest son Jacob. Jacob had just started attending Sonoma University in California. Having just moved to Rohnert Park for his junior year, after attending community college, he bought a two-bedroom condo to live in. He knew he would need a roommate to share the expenses of homeownership.

He interviewed different people through the first month of school, without finding a match. At that point, an unmarried couple applied to rent the room. Jacob interviewed them and during their discussion, he found out they had a child and another baby on the way. The man was not working and the woman was about to start her maternity leave. To top everything off, they had been evicted before. Jacob's heart was feeling for them as he talked with them both.

He called to tell me about his potential new roommates. Or so I thought. He asked me what my thoughts were on having them stay. I instantly said, "No, do not do that. Do they have family in the area? Let them go live with their family. You are asking for problems."

Jacob said, "It is too late. I told them, 'Yes!'"

"No," I said. "Tell them that things have changed and that I said, 'No.'"

"Dad, you taught me to stand by my word. I gave them my word."

I sighed, "Ok. It is your place. You handle it. Just let me know how it goes, and if you need anything else."

In December, I got a call from my sister, Anita. She told me that Jacob asked to borrow some money from her. Earlier that week, she recommended that he talk with me about the circumstances. Wanting to know if Jacob did, she called me. I told her that he hadn't.

She explained that the roommates had not given Jacob any money after the first day they moved in. He had to drop some of his classes to work more in order to pay the mortgage and not lose his place. She expanded on the situation, sharing that Jacob had also gotten a restraining order against the man after being assaulted by him. Jacob had been to court, trying to evict the roommates, but he was getting nowhere. The roommates knew the loopholes in the judicial system.

Now, being an upset father, I drove the hour over to the condo, to meet the roommates, Gary and Lisa, for myself. During the drive, I started praying about what to do and when I arrived I heard these words: "Bless them."

The guy was there, sitting on the steps leading to the second floor entrance. I introduced myself and got directly to the point. I asked him when he would leave peacefully, without being evicted. Gary's response was that he wasn't leaving. He had no place to take his family. I responded, "My son is going to lose his home because of you, and *he* will be homeless, so you need to leave!"

I asked Gary, "Tell me, what it would take to get you out of the condo?" I offered him five hundred dollars, as a blessing.

Tensions were building as we talked. Gary stood up as if he was going to assault me. Looking him in the eyes, I shook my head and said to myself, "Don't be stupid."

The Gary was infuriated. Turning back into the condo, he lashed out, "You can't make me move!"

I turned to leave, frustrated. As I headed back home, I talked to the Lord asking Him, "What to do?"

A week went by as I continued seeking the Lord. I told to Him, "What You said to do didn't work. I need your help!"

During that week, I tried to pray a prayer of intercession over Gary, Lisa and their family, to break off some things I had seen over them. I felt for their children and the families of others that would be affected by their curses. I understood that these curses had been handed down from generation to generation; the cycle needed to be broken. As I started interceding in prayer, I heard the Lord say, "You have no authority!"

I stopped dead in my tracks.

During the week that followed, Gary continued to assault Jacob. Police intervention was required. Jacob could easily have defended himself, having been trained in martial arts. But, he refused to resort to violence. Jacob moved back home, and began commuting to class and work each day while Gary and Lisa stayed in his condo, not paying anything. My biker friends who knew what was happening wanted to go and throw them out, but I refused, telling them, "No, I will handle it."

The next week, Dan McCollam, associate pastor at The Mission Church, was going to Willits, California to speak at a church. I joined the team that was going with him. The trip to Willits would lead us right through Rhonert Park, and two hours beyond. I took my own car and drove alone, with the intention of stopping at the condo on the way back. I still had no idea what I would do. While driving, spoke with God, listening and watching for an answer.

We made it to Willits and enjoyed a phenomenal service. God orchestrated some divine meetings and released many accurate visions and prophesies through us. It was an awesome experience, but when it ended, I knew it was time to start the drive home: the drive to the condo.

As I was driving and talking to the Lord, I heard, "I said for you to bless them."

I replied, "I tried but the man said no."

The next words I heard inhabited my spirit, transforming my thoughts and the way I viewed things from an earthly to a heavenly perspective. I heard, "Bless them the way you would your own son if he was in that situation."

That was something that I would not have considered. It was not a concept I had grown up with, being raised the way I had. I now knew what I needed to do when I reached the condo.

When I arrived, I sat in my SUV and wrote a check. Not just any check. I wrote a check to Gary that I would have given Jacob, my own son, if he had been in that situation. I knocked on the door. Gary and Lisa were home and I talked with them outside on the porch balcony. I showed them the check, which had a number and a few zeros on it. Then I asked, "When I bless you with this money, when will you be gone?"

Gary replied, "Right after Christmas," which was only two weeks away. I finished filling out both of their full names on the check, handed it to them, got back in my car and left. On the drive back home, I heard this:

"You now have authority."

I thanked the Lord and told Him, "I put my trust in You Lord." I knew the authority given to me enabled me to now speak life and break off the curses that clung to them. I understood that that the power had come when they accepted the money. I had invested in them, loved them and as they received it, they gave me clearance to speak into their lives, breaking off the curses on their family.[21] Where I had no authority, I gained authority by loving them like a father, and their acceptance of the blessing brought more than any of us could imagine.

This exchange allowed the release of prayers for many things: protection for the children and a better life with favor, grace and mercy, included. Standing in the gap, dealing with generational curses is a seer's obligation and part of his or her destiny, as led by the Holy Spirit. I continued in prayer until I ran out of things to pray for. At that point, I found myself being ten minutes from home.

Later that week I stopped by the Christian book store and purchased a "Children's Precious Moments Bible" for their kids. I gave it to Jacob to give to Gary and Lisa as a Christmas gift for their children.

---

21 Matthew 16: 19: "I will give you the keys of the kingdom of heaven, and whatever you bind on earth shall be bound in heaven and whatever you loose on earth shall be loosed in heaven."

Right after Christmas, I drove up to the condo. Gary was sitting on the steps. I asked if everything was out of the condo. He retorted, "No, I cannot get into a new place until January 1."

Looking Gary dead in the eyes I reminded him, "You promised." I paused for moment and finished, "I will be back here January first and I expect you to be gone."

On my way home that day, I only had a simple prayer: "Lord I tried it Your way. You have to do it. That's it. I have tried it Your way. You have to do it." That is all I prayed the whole ride home.

As New Year's Day and the final drive to condo approached, I kept telling Jacob and Lorrie, "The Lord has this. They will be gone."

When I reached the condo, I found that Lisa had been moving everything out of the condo with her girlfriend. Gary was in Redding, California, about four hours away. His brother had come to help Lisa move the large furniture.

Talking with Jacob, I learned he had not yet given them the Children's Bible. He brought it to me, and gave me the pleasure of giving it to Lisa. Though she didn't show much of an outward response, she shared that she had never owned a Bible and that she would read it to her children. The atmosphere over that mother was changing as the curses were vanishing. A short time later, the family was gone from condo and there was a fresh start for everyone.

Jacob got his condo back, and found a good roommate shortly thereafter. Because of kindness in Jacob's heart, it took him a semester longer than he had planned to graduate with a Bachelors of Science Degree in Physiological Biology.

A JACOB HEART

Jacob was the first grandchild in his family, on both his parent's sides, to get a college degree.

I was proud that Jacob upheld his word, even in the face of all it cost him. His word and promises are a personification of who he is. I believe the Lord saw Jacob's heart[22] as he was being deceived and as he chose to uphold his word still upholding his word and keep his promise. The Lord took pleasure in him and showed Himself faithful in how He took care of Jacob in the months that followed.

Over time, Jacob rectified the finances on the condo and did not lose his property. He eventually got a modification from the bank on the money owed them. He repaid all the people he had borrowed from to keep the condo. I found out later he had sold many of his childhood collectables on EBay to repay what he owed. That is integrity!

These acts of Jacob reminded me of the story of the Gibeonites when Joshua gave them a promise after being deceived by them (Joshua 9). He stood his ground and kept the promise he gave in the Lord's name. Centuries later, King David had to avenge what happened to the Gibeonites, because God upheld Joshua's promise (2 Samuel 21). God takes promises very seriously.

God took Jacob's promise and set a family free of curses by opening a door of favor, blessings and abundance for them and their children. It was a picture illustration of how God takes any bad situation and turns it into good.[24]

---

22 Romans 8:27: "And he who searches hearts knows what is the mind of the Spirit, because the Spirit intercedes for the saints according to the will of God."

24 Romans 8:28: "And we know that for those who love God all things work together for good, for those who are called according to his purpose."

In my own life, He opened the door of good for me, transforming my mind so I could understand and operate from a Kingdom understanding of Jesus Christ's love and what He wants for each of us. We are to do this for one another.

> *A new commandment I give you, that you Love one another just as I have loved you, you also are to love on another. By this all people will know you are mine, if you have love for one another* (John 13:34-35).

We just have to be willing to have the eyes of our heart opened to see, to look, and to hear what God is saying.

LOOKING BACK

Even now, as I reflect back on this event years later, I am still growing from my son's heart and the love of Christ. Jacob's necessity for roommate and Gary's needs for his family were simply facts of circumstance and desires.

It is the intentions of their hearts that can today reveal their actions as good or bad.

Jacob's need of a roommate was for financial stability. It was a necessity. So was Gary and Lisa's need of a place for their family to live. Their choices arose from their need, though there were spiritual forces at work, battling. This is one reason why the Holy Spirit searches the hearts, mind and spirit of man to know the true intentions of each one.[25]

---

25 1 Corinthians 2:10.

Jacob's compassion added to his own need overturned wisdom. He overlooked natural knowledge, and maybe even common sense, in his choice. We all have done this to some degree. Unfortunately, not all circumstances come out with God's peace; but they can if we are willing to trust in Him.

If not for the Lord, the act of loving with the Father's love would have been far from my thoughts, and the breakthrough may not have come. If I had ignored the word spoken to me, and had not acted on it with faith and works, I could have created a wrong outcome for all.

When a difficult situation arises in your life, as it did in ours, stop and take a moment. Perhaps kneel down and rest; your answer could be found in something as simple as asking for help. There is always an answer that can be found if we are willing to step out of our "box".

Remember: Be transformed from worldly formats and perspectives by allowing God to reformat within you a Kingdom mentality, with a heart after Christ for new encoding.[26]

Also, remember, it is not our place to judge a person. It is our job to use wisdom and knowledge on how to handle each situation, with the help of the Holy Spirit.

---

26 Ephesians 4:22-24.

CHAPTER 4

NOBLE SAINTS OF ANCIENT TIMES

THERE ARE NECESSITIES IN our DNA make-up, things we have a need, drive or desire for, that are seen in our emotional activity and spiritual characteristic. These necessities have purpose, shown throughout time.

During an evening secession of soaking in the Lord's presence at The Mission, parts of our spiritual DNA structure presented themselves. The group was practicing a type of contemplative prayer, laying down or sitting listening to soft Christian music that we were just being quiet with no praying, except for a simple one or two-line prayer of, "I'm waiting on You, God, in Jesus name." We each kept a note pad and pencil at our side to write down those things that came to mind. This allowed us to just relax and hear what the Lord was speaking, while being able to document what He was saying.

It was during this time that I had a vision. In the beginning of the vision I saw human skulls of various sizes and shapes flying through the air at me and past me, like in a movie. I believed that these skulls, which also encompassed body parts, such as a ligaments and femurs, represented different ages of time passing. I noticed that some of the skulls were moving in pairs together; I assumed that these were couples or partners. They would just appear, coming and going, from entirely different expanses of the vision.

Then I began to wonder, "Have I tapped into an unclean source?"

I tried to shake the vision, then to rebuke it, as it stayed. Then, wanting to make sure unclean forces were not trying to tap into my streaming lines of communication, I asked for intervention from the Holy Spirit. I started testing the vision; I began to think about what I saw and what was happening, while asking the Lord what it was about.[27]

As peace began to settle within, bringing calmness over me, the skulls changed to men holding, carrying, and dragging crosses. I saw each one's face. The vision then made sense; it was showing times past, individuals and couples carrying their crosses with joy in adversity.

As I went deeper in observation, these were the affairs I saw:

The first face that took focus was that of a middle-aged man. He had a beard and a crown on his head. He was wearing a beautiful, royal robe like those worn by royalty in ancient times.

Then I saw another, next to him, coming closer. He looked very old and fragile at first glance. His beard went down to his knees. His eyes where full of knowledge and truth that could be seen as well as felt. Examining him closer, I saw that his body structure was as solid, firm and full of strength as a man in his prime. It was his clothing that carried the fragile look hanging about him. Then, I observed that this old one carried the cross with such ease, it was

---

27 1 John 4:1: "...test the spirits...."

as though he and the cross were one. His crown looked like it was an embodiment of him, which is why I didn't notice it at first, sitting nobly upon his head.

During all of this, I was surveying the others, some close by and some in the distance. They ranged in age from youths to elders. The men had beards of different lengths that seemed to have significance, yet to be revealed. Each one I observed resembled nobles of ancient times. Those with longer beards exuded an essence of integrity, grace, and humility as they all looked at me with their crowns that seemed to be hidden, yet radiating brilliance.

In another area, a group of both men and women, dressed in majestic clothing, were standing in a half circle. I saw no crowns on them. They were kneeling on one knee, with the exception of the nobleman closest to me, who had a counseling presence that radiated from him, carrying an elevated authority. I could see power stream out of him in waves, as in the form of body heat. He turned his head and looked up at me with a smile. It was as if he was in prayer or bowing. I saw him speaking to me, though I heard nothing. Nevertheless, I sensed something happening inside me.

Moving towards us, closing the distance to our right, was a man carrying- perhaps dragging – no, carrying his cross on his back in one flowing motion. He was smiling from ear-to-ear; the closer he came, the bigger the smile widened. The face of the cross was brilliantly bright, pointing to sky. The back side of the cross was touching his back and was like a gleaming, illuminated, copper-gold.

I perceived the faces of the men, women and children that were coming and going in all directions at the beginning of the vision. The majority of faces were bold and exquisite in appearance.

Then, the intense brilliance of the cross caught my attention. I turned my head, trying to gaze back at it. The inner luminescence of the cross had some kind of form, but I could not see it. It was blinding.

Instantly, I returned back to the soaking session. Immediately, I tried to describe the ethereal meeting in writing in an attempt to record and relate what I had just seen.

This vision kept returning over and over in the following months, progressively bringing clarity to itself. It also released impartation from the Noble Saints, releasing what they had received to me, for others.

There are impartations and anointing from older times, waiting to be released for future callings that still await us now. They come from those who carried their crosses as we now carry ours. They impart to the saints of today what was given to them.

TSUNAMI RELEASE

A couple months passed since the Noble Saints and I had just finished reading a book, *Releasing the Angel Breakthrough*.[28] I had just returned from a mission trip to India. The contents of this book rested in my spirit, and I felt a tug to see the author- Paul Keith Davis.

Shortly thereafter, I discovered that Paul Keith was putting on a conference called, "Releasing the Angel Breakthrough." It was short notice and I would be registering late, but I knew that I had to go. I checked in with Lorrie, and getting her "go" on the idea,

---

28 Davis, Paul Keith. *Releasing the Angel Breakthrough*, April 2006. White Dove Ministries, www.whitedoveministries.org.

I packed my bags. The guest speakers included Bob Jones, Bobby Connor, Shawn Bolz, Randy Demain, and John Kilpatrick, with worship by Joanne McFatter.

Now, I'm always concerned if I'm on the right course. I like to check and double check my decisions with the Lord. But, over time, I've learned that when you step out with the right heart, you can't get it wrong; that kind of faith brings favor. Sometimes favor doesn't come until you are fully committed or even en-route. This time, favor showed up as I stepped out to make my plans, with no time to spare. I was able to book a direct flight, straight through to Mobile, Alabama and upon arrival at the airport, Hertz car rental upgraded me from a small to a midsize luxury car. The local hotels were fully booked, but there was a last-minute cancellation which opened up a room for me, right down the street from the conference. They even gave me a discount! But still, the most exciting part of all of this was getting to share the hotel elevator with the hosts: Paul Keith and Wanda Davis.

The next day, I rose early to see what the Lord was saying before heading out for the day. The conference started and it was packed; more chairs were brought in and set around the auditorium walls. It was during Joanne's third worship song that the atmosphere ignited, bringing actual encounters.

Then, out of the blue, I was translated to a mountaintop. I found myself standing on snow skis with the Lord standing on the back of them. Here, I could feel, as well as respond to, everything that was happening all around. The two of us were skiing down the mountain and it seemed like the slopes themselves where moving, but not moving, as if we were one in movement with the slopes.

Then abruptly, the two of us went from being on the skis together, to our own snowboards. We were doing extreme, wild, crazy, fun things on those snowboards. The Lord was showing me how to spin in the air as we caught air. We were going upside down, spinning around, flipping loops and more! I was being instructed on how to stand, when to lean forward or backward as different terrains presented themselves on the mountain.

Then the snowboard altered its shape under my feet and it became bigger more rounded as a ship rudder for steering, cutting through the snow. It accelerated faster and faster heading downhill. I started getting nervous, yet excited with a bit of fear, at the speed in which it was traveling but without great control.

Suddenly, the Lord was on the board behind me, saying, "Don't worry. I'm with you." He continued, "Lean backwards, not forward on this section." I understood that this meant to rest on Him, and let Him take control.

Now, I was steering this board with only the feel of the terrain under my feet; my vision was obscured because of the speed at which we were moving. Not having a clear, visual picture of what was ahead was difficult for me. I had to trust and give up control. I believed that if I leaned over to try and see what was up ahead, I would possibly crash, so instead, I chose to hold on to His words to me. The fear left as I put my trust in Him. I continued feeling my way speedily down the hill. We were having a blast together.

The two of us began to catch air again. On the second or third jump, the board transformed once more. We were on our own surfboards, now show-jumping large ocean waves. We rode next to one another, with me on His right side. I noticed that the crest of the wave we were riding was hitting the shore. I rode the wave right onto the shore and hopped off the board. Turning my head, I saw the Lord had spun His board around just before it hit shoreline and headed back out into the ocean to catch another wave. I heard these words:

"Are you going to stay there, just watching as history goes by, lingering on past memories?"

Pausing amidst the great fun, I pondered those words. You see, there are changes of seasons and equipment in our lives, and they come with the knowledge that is needed as our perspectives and authority grow. New knowledge brings in resources that are activated when we receive them and walk, putting our trust in the Lord. We can live in past achievements and hold ourselves back from advancing, or we can whip ourselves around, learn something new, and catch the next level of power being released, though it will be beyond our present understanding.

I grabbed my board and ran back into the water. I jumped on the board and I followed the Lord. Another wave came on the way out, but it was smaller than the one before. I started to turn to catch the wave, but the Lord said, "No, not that one." Then as the wave came we went right though it, under the wave, under the water, still standing on the boards.

The thing that got me was this: When you head out to catch a wave in the natural, you paddle your way out, working hard to catch the wave. It was not so in this experience. The Lord showed me how to enjoy riding out to catch the wave, not working to get out there and being exhausted when the waves finally come. I believe some have been so tired they've missed the joy of riding the wave of life. They have become exhausted in plowing through life, plowing through spiritual battles, that they've missed the fun. They miss out on relationship with Christ. They struggle to the moment of breakthrough, and when it finally comes, there is no joy in the moment. They have no energy left to take pleasure in the good thing God is releasing to them in that moment.

We stayed under the water, riding farther and farther out, to catch the next wave. It seemed like forever, but nonetheless, things began to shift. I also noticed that we were breathing underwater. It was awesome! On top of learning to ride through the water with the Lord, I began to understand how to breathe the water. As we talked, I kept asking questions and received answers that prompted more questions. At this time, I found myself observing myself with the Lord; I could not hear the questions or the answers being spoken. It was as if it was muted. This was an impartation, but I couldn't hear all of it because a part of my spirit had to wait for the appointed time of release.

As the Lord spoke, the words He used and the things He revealed were illuminating me in the vision as I watched. I looked like a little child asking, "Why?" and "How come?" and "Let me try! Let me try!" I now realize that the teaching was also in what I was seeing, not just hearing, from the Lord.[29]

Then, I caught these words, unmuted: "It is time."

The two of us came up out of the water on the back of a huge tidal wave and began surfing on top of it. Within moments, we

---

29 Habakkuk 2:1.

were joined by Josiah, my youngest son. He was surfing on my right followed by his two brothers, Jacob and Joshua. To my left was Lorrie, with many others joining them on both the right and left side of the huge crest of a wave. The line of people extended as far as the eye could see along the top of the wave crest. All were on surfboards.

While we were riding on the crest of the wave the Lord told me go into the peak of the tunnel. The next moment, I pushed my board down, going straight down through the crest, coming out riding the inside arch of the tunnel, upside down. I was no longer observing myself; I was now in the pike, feeling the water all around, on my skin, the mist in my face and adrenaline flowing through my body. It was both exhilarating and rejuvenating. After a moment I was observing myself again. During this experience, I was continually translated back and forth from watching to participating, from the vision, or daydream, to some other place. Only the Lord knows what this really was. This continued to happen for some time as I was riding the inside peak.

Hearing the instruction to, "Ride it higher on the inside of the crest peak," I responded by cutting deeper into the tunnel as it formed the wave crest. I cut in and out of the arch of the crest as the others were still riding on the top of the peak. The faster I cut into the curve of the arch, the higher the peak would rise. Again I heard, "Cut into it." I carved even deeper into the tunnel arch and the peak of the tsunami got larger. My carving was sculpting the wave like a knife fashioning a deep mold for a crown.

I yelled for the others on top to follow me, shaping patterns into the crest as we were spinning in the arch like a precision drill coming out behind the peak, in a line on the wave. The peak was now a resolute tsunami in size.

I heard again: "It is time." I turned into the tsunami and the others followed in a line formation. The person directly behind me followed my every motion and action. Those behind followed suit, copying the actions and motions of the one in front of them, each doing what the other did while riding, creating the tsunami.

Now all of us were surfing under the water, gathering momentum with a new mobility and power. As they came out of the water, the astonishment on their faces contained a mixture of joy, boldness and fearlessness that could not be expressed in mere words. Then, on top of the water, the surfboards spun 180-degrees around, and began heading up to the crest of the tsunami.

The top of the crest so high up, you could barely see the water directly below. Just above the tsunami were huge white clouds, with one enormous cloud of mist and sea foam staying just ahead of the tsunami path. As I glanced to my right and left, I noticed that all were enjoying riding the tsunami's crest.

The season upon us brings new abilities, creativity, boldness and greater achievements, where we will do what was said to be impossible. These actions will create a seismic wave, if we are ready to commit ourselves to joining with God's Kingdom. Currently, from the natural perspective, this means having no fear of stepping into the realm that the saints have been given control of to bring truth and life.

Then, with a flash, everything changed. We were where no longer riding surfboards. The boards had been changed to wave riders. Each person was riding one, standing on it as if it was a jet ski. They were all gripping the handles with extreme strength as the accelerating G-forces pushed their smiles from ear to ear. It reminded me of a Warner-Brothers cartoon, where Wyle E. Coyote was tied to a rocket and launched; we were going mach speed!

In investigating tsunamis, after this experience, I discovered that the "power of the tsunami is determined by the amount by which the sea floor is displaced. Similarly, the wavelength and period of the tsunami are determined by the size and shape of the underwater disturbance. The tsunami's energy flux, which is dependent on both its wave speed and wave height, remains nearly constant. Consequently, as the tsunami's speed diminishes, its height grows".[30] The acceleration of our travel was needed to keep up at the speed the crest of the tsunami, to keep the wave moving.

Observing again, I saw the Spirit of the Lord as in Isaiah 11:2.

> *The Spirit of the Lord shall rest upon him, the Spirit of wisdom, Spirit of understanding, Spirit of counsel, Spirit of might, the Spirit of knowledge and the fear of the Lord.*

I saw that the parts of His Spirit (wisdom, understanding, counsel, might, knowledge and fear of the Lord) were attached to each other. They also seemed to be simultaneously holding on to me as I was being rocketed along and floating in the air in as colors and presence all at the same time.

---

[30] Australian Government Bureau of Meteorology, www.bom.gov.au/tsunami/info/.

I saw the Lord's Spirit outlined in specific colors. From where I stood, observing myself through the mist, several colors stood out to me. The ones that stood out the most, were the Red Spirit which is Wisdom, then the Yellow or Golden Spirit which Knowledge, followed by the Blue Spirit or Indigo Spirit, which represent the Fear of the Lord and Might, though I couldn't quite determine which color I was seeing.[32]

The mist engulfing me was vivid in its presence. I knew there was meaning in the mist.[33] In researching the Scriptures, I found that Hebrew meaning of the word for "mist" is dynamic. It can mean giving life or releasing abundance, refer to God fulfilling His Word, the rising up of a leader or leaders, teachers (ministers, scientist, doctors, etc.), or to clean the fruit or harvest floors. This is what I was seeing in the vision: the rising up of leaders.

I continued to examine the Spirits as they seemed to take on human-type shapes, with hands and arms. Then they began to merge into me. I knew then that the Lord had big plans ahead, things that we could not do on our own but only with Him.

Looking into the sky, I noticed that the foam was changing into a big white dove, and from there, into many doves. At times it seemed like they were a combination of doves and a flaming eagle streaking through the sky.

At that moment the foam reached back took ahold of me, flipped me up and forward, high into the air. I was thrown midway

---

[32] For more information, Isaiah 11:2, www.WhiteDoveMinistries.org, Paul Keith Davis.

[33] Job 36:27-28, Jeremiah 10:13, James 4:14. See also the Appendix.

between the heavens and the peak of the tsunami crest, far inland. The mist followed, hovering, held or floating in midair, observing. Likewise, I could do nothing but watch what was about to happen from high above, neither in Heaven nor on the wave.

I saw that the riders could control were the crest would put them ashore; they had a choice. They began to make their ways to different places. There were some who rode the tsunami inland while the others rode only to shoreline, as the peak broke in places, according to the topography around the globe.

The first half to split away from the group rode the tsunami deep inland to different locations. I saw some in cities, mountains, towns, farms, and coastal regions. Those that came inland at different spots were received by all nationalities of men and women. Some of those just stood around with people that lived there trying to decide, "What to do next?" The second half split again, as the first half did, heading back out to catch another wave.

Suddenly, I was returned back to the conference. I had no awareness of anything that been happening in the natural. With my eyes open I stood, turned around and facing away from the stage, I surveyed my surroundings. It was all I could do before reengaging in the worship service, entirely entrenched in the Kingdom presence.

The riders in this vision are individuals being released to teach the nations, that they may understand what God is saying and doing in this present age. Their job will be to teach those who do not see so that they may see what He is doing and hear what is said. They will work together with others who also see, hear, feel and know to release the full Gospel of Jesus Christ, for the advancement of the Kingdom of God. They will release sparks in the Spirit, igniting fires as they take hold of their spiritual gifts and their personal authority and power.[35]

We must take ourselves and others to new levels of power and authority in the Spirit. We must be willing to be a friend, be a protector to those in need; when we do this, military strategies are released to us. As we endeavor on this journey, embrace the knowledge that the Lord is with you as your Friend, Brother, Captain and King. He is our Lord, the Lord of lords. He will supply us with every good a perfect gift needed to accomplish His purposes in our time.

THE SWORDS

The next day followed with speakers Bob Jones, Paul Keith and Bobby Conner. During worship that day, I went into another ethereal vision.

I saw myself receiving a new sword from the Lord. It looked like the sword I had to leave behind in India, with the Global Awakening team.[36] also received a staff, matching the sword in color. They were both golden, with burnt gold in the hilt. When I received the staff, I heard, "Carry this staff, just as Moses had carried his."

I knew this had global implications in space, time, people and places.

As I observed the staff, the end started changing shape to a spearhead, a torch and also something like a globe on the top, floating in the middle of two rings that where spinning. The staff

---

35 John 16:13-14, 1 Corinthians 12:11.

36 Santos, Ramon. *Chronicles of a Seer,* Chapter 13.

changed back again to its original shape with color that again harmonized with the sword.

Then I saw another vision within that vision. I was holding the sword, and the Lord was showing me how it had been, and was still being forged, conveying strength to its composition. The sword was in my hand during the forging epoch, as the golden color was transforming. The colors on the blade and the hilt amalgamated in composition. It was getting larger and stronger, becoming more resilient and though it looked heavier, it got lighter. Its very appearance was one having its own virtues and integrity encompassed in it.

The sword got brighter until it became a very bright, white light. It then became transparent in appearance, having just an outline of laser-sharp edges. The outline vanished then rematerialized as a burnt golden color of a refined gold, but enhanced.

Just before the first vision faded, I was given three more staffs and swords that corresponded to each other, shadowed by a few more swords of a different type.

The vision within the vision was gone.

I knew these weapons to be impartations for other saints in the Kingdom. Each had a different gift of authority and power, yet all worked together in the release of the Kingdom, setting people free from the strongholds of the enemy.

As I was released from the vision, I had to kneel down on one knee in the conference, needing to rest from the weight of what had just happened. It was as if much of my strength had left. Again, I was so consumed by what had just been released in *ethereal* visions that all I could do in response to the rest of the conference was just sit and give my yes and amen.

CHAPTER 5

EMBRACING DESIGN AND STAR OF GRACE

AS WE EACH EMBRACE our own design, with love for others, we will mature. This is a need that many of us carry; loving others is a natural, internal desire. However, we need to intentionally step into it because love will not happen on its own. This is something that we all need to do, as you will see in the following story.

One year after the conference visions, Lorrie and I were on a tight travel schedule. We caught three training schools in one month, each one overlapping the next. That month we caught the last four days of the "School of the Prophets" at Bethel Church in Redding, California, ran to the airport and jumped on a plane to Toronto, Canada. There was a Healing School at Toronto Airport Christian Fellowship (TACF), now called Catch the Fire (CTF). The teachers were Randy Clark who known for global healings and Ché Ahn, the head pastor of Harvest Rock Church in Pasadena, California. I have had the privilege to take missions trips with Randy to Brazil and India. Both are godly leaders who walk in supernatural healings.

During one of the teaching sessions, Randy surprised us by announcing that we were going to hear testimonies about what Jesus Christ was doing on mission trips, with those willing to step out. Well, he didn't necessarily surprise *us*. But he did surprise *me* when he called me to the platform to share! I testified about the Brazilian man whose leg was broken in three places and had never completely healed. The Lord aligned and restored his leg in all of its three broken spots.[37]

The week was inspirational and it added to our corporate knowledge of supernatural healings, both today and in the past. TACF was expecting a large group: 250 pastors and leaders from Norway and about 150 others, to give a total of 400 people. The amazing thing about these Norwegians was that all of them had had all of their expenses paid for by a Norwegian businessman, who was also attending the conference. He wanted his country, Norway, to experience the Father's heart, the expression being released in Toronto.

TRAIN THE TRAINERS AND RANDY MCKENZIE

As the Healing School ended we concluded it was worth the push we endured to get there. One of the most impactful experiences we had at TACF was the charismatic ministry training, where we learning to minister the Father's love for all. This training, dubbed, "Train the Trainers," was primarily for pastors and leaders. This was an intense curriculum on the love of the Father's heart. This "Train the Trainers" event coordinated divine connections, relationships, opportunities and grace beyond comprehension. After

---

37 Santos, Ramon. *Chronicles of a Seer*, Chapter 11.

graduation, the group would go through a ministry gifting evaluation, to help TACF and CTF create teams for greater fruitfulness in outreach.

The week-long training was exceptional in what it revealed on the love and heart of the Father. It was upon entering the training facility that evening that Lorrie and I saw Michael and Leslie Martin, friends we had made the previous year at the soaking school at TACF. Michael grabbed me, saying, "I have someone for you to meet!" as he led us into one of the classrooms.

I saw him immediately, amidst the crowd. The guy had an incredible, spiritual atmosphere around him as he was laying hands on people. I observed bolts of lightning being released through the palms of his hands, into people who then fell to the floor. Michael brought him over to us and introduced us, saying, "This is Randy McKenzie." As Randy and I reached out to shake hands, just before our palms touched, there was an explosion between our hands. Both of us recoiled from the surge of power. It was like the crossing of electrical currents.

This was the start of a great friendship. After we were able to get ourselves up off the floor, we spent that night laying hands on people, watching them fall under the power of the Holy Spirit. A few flew across the room. When those that were struck got back up, they would invariably announce that their ailments and infirmities had been completely healed, without a single word of knowledge or healing prayer.

Thank You, Jesus! Amen.

We spent the evening bragging about what the Holy Spirit was doing while playing catch with fireballs in the spirit realms. These spiritual fireballs were full of power that could be tossed, as though a natural ball, and given to recipients, resulting in manifestations of physical healing, doors of breakthrough and opportunity opening in natural, releases of peace and joy, and more.[38]

I listened as Randy told the story of how the Lord had restored his health after five years of being disabled with rods, cables, and pins in his back and spine. This is documented as a medical miracle by third parties[39] and can be viewed on a DVD, YouTube, and the news. It is called "The Randy McKenzie Story."[40] The metal in his body had completely disappeared without any surgery, even the parts of metal that had fused to his spine. It was the Finger of God at work. The two of us spent our time together at this event, being almost inseparable.

At the graduation dinner, everything changed. The ambiance shifted; the atmosphere felt sweeter and alive with movement. The Senior Leaders of TACF, John and Carol Arnott, Duncan and Sarah Smith, with Steve and Sandra Long had everyone line up for impartations from all the leaders. Unexpectedly, I saw and felt the heavenly atmosphere transform again, becoming much like the calm before a storm. Then I spotted a vortex stirring in the heavens, through the ceiling, as the presence of the Lord came in.

THE STAR OF GRACE

Entering the shift was like stepping out of a swimming pool of cool water and diving into the clear, blue, warm water of the Caribbean Ocean, where life swims all around you.

---

38 Santos, Ramon. *Chronicles of a Seer*, Chapter 10.

39 www.explorationfilms.com/explorationfilms-RandyMcKenzie.html.

40 teamfamilyonline.com/miracles-randy-mckenzie-story-5year-update/.

The vortex I saw coming through the roof took on the appearance of a star as it moved through the room. I named it the "Star of Grace." The star was twinkling like one in the night sky. I watched in amazement as it came across the ceiling to rest above John's head, then floated down, ever so gently, settling in his left hand.

I have always believed that if you can see it, you can have it. This principle is in the Scriptures:

> *The secret things belong to the Lord our God, but the things that are revealed belong to us and to our children forever, that we may do all the words of this law* (Deuteronomy 29:29).

We are to love one another as we would love ourselves, in order to improve and grow, making this a better world. Is this not what science and humanity is all about? Is this not what is in the hearts of scholars? Surely it is. The Scriptures tell us that we were born to search for answers:

> *It is the glory of God to conceal things, but the glory of kings is to search things out* (Proverbs 25:2).

As everyone was lining up for the impartation, we jumped to the first of the lines. Lorrie was second in our line, I became the third. There were three lines, with thirty-five or more people in each line.

As John and Carol laid hands on the first two people, they dropped to the floor like heavy bricks. John touched my hands, dropping me to one knee from the power of the anointing that was released and imparted to me. It took all I had to stay on that one knee. I did not want to fall out under the power. I told myself, "I am not going to miss out on what they carry."

But, when Carol laid hands on me next, I wasn't sure if I would make it. The feeling was like the impact of being hit by a freight train, slamming me face-first into the ground. I tried to keep focused on the Star of Grace that was given to John as he became a blur, passing down the line. I tried to get up, to no avail, because of the weight of the presence. It took every ounce of my strength to even try to focus on remembering, "If you can see it you can have it." To me, this was just as it was with Elijah being taken to Heaven: "If you see me taken, it is yours, Elisha." (This account is recorded in 2 Kings 2.) I was not going to let this slip by; I wanted that gift!

I began praying, "Lord, I don't want to miss out on anything that is happening right now. Please don't let me miss out on what is being given at this moment. I am going after that 'Star of Grace' that I see."

The more I tried to get up, the heavier the weight resting on me became. I was being pressed to the ground and there was nothing I could do to change it. I began seeing visions, with words beyond comprehension being released, in both spiritual realms and natural sight. They came at a nearly incomprehensible rate; I could not keep up with the speed at which I was receiving these revelations. When I could finally look up, the leaders were on the last line. Still unable to stand, I crawled on my stomach, like in military combat training, to the end of the last line. I continually prayed, "I do not want to miss out on that 'Star of Grace!'"

As John, Carol and the others got closer I gathered enough strength to stand. Or, perhaps, did the Presence let me get up?

I do not know. This time, Carol was the first to impart. As the palms of her hands were about to touch the palms of my hands, electricity arched across the gap like bolts of lightning, flowing like the current of a river. I don't know how I managed to stay on my feet, especially when I saw all of the grace emanating from her. I felt like a ship on a stormy ocean; I was being tossed in all directions.

When John came as I began stuttering in speech, trying to speak to him. He asked what I had said.

"Sir," I said, "I saw Grace given to your left hand."

He asked again, "What did you say?"

I repeated, "I saw grace given into your left hand, and I believe if you can see it, you can have it.'"

I fell to one knee from the power of storm within and around me, this time managing to stay upright. John reached down, took my left hand and held it open. "Take it, take it, take it!" he declared, smacking his hand down hard on mine, palm to palm, left hand to left hand. Instantly, there was an implosion of power released into me. I dropped head first onto the ground, laying there incoherent from the magnitude of what was delivered. I can even feel it now as I write.

The Star of Grace was recoiling throughout my body. I don't know how long I stayed in my position on the ground. When I could stand again- much, much, later- I felt the endowment of grace throbbing in my left hand.

Back at the hotel that night, I had continual pulsations of pain. The enrichment of the impartation resonated within me. It was as though I was growing as I was being brought in and out ethereal and actual experiences and elements. These experiences of the spiritual realms were new to me.

I do not know if I had closed my eyes, but when I laid my head down on my pillow, I remembered these words:

> *For God speaks in one way, and in two, though man does not perceive it. In a dream, in a vision of the night, when deep sleep falls on men, while they slumber on their beds* (Job 33:14-15).

> *I bless the Lord who gives me counsel; in the night* (Psalm 16:7).

KEYS FROM A WHISPERING GOD

The experience with the Star of Grace had released spiritual gifts of grace from the Holy Spirit. The power of God was released as these words were released in the actual dream and/or visions. After having this encounter, I sought wisdom, knowledge and understanding on the proclamations, knowing these were greater than I knew. I recorded the night's events and shared them with other Christians: Bryan Easterling, a seer,[41] Phyllis Miller, a dream interpreter[42] and Steve Carpenter, a theologian.[43]

It is essential that you seek to see and hear what God is saying. It is a gift; it belongs to you and your children forever. God's Spirit speaks to us in many ways. The Spirit reveals to us, and our spirit,

---

41 Byron Easterling: bhhinc.org.
42 The Dream Team: destined2dream.com.
43 Steve Carpenter: christianfellowshipministry.org.

His love and the destiny that He wants for us through the desires of our hearts and through love for one another. God allows the Holy Spirit to release in us authority and power, through Jesus Christ, to accomplish these heavenly desires. When our hearts and minds are open to this reality, the essence released from us is grace.

GRACE

Two sets of keys were given in the Spirit during the visions of that night of impartation. They looked of ancient times. One set was much larger than the other and seemed to be older; that set contained two keys. The next set was a smaller ring with three keys on it. Both sets were on large key rings that held the keys.

As I looked, a ring of royalty, or signet ring, followed. It started as a ruby and continued to change to different stones, such as sapphire, amethyst, diamond, and a couple of other stones that I didn't recognize.

I put the two key rings onto my left arm. They joined to become an inner and outer ring with space between them, except where they connected in a couple spots. They were just like the spirals that go around a globe. The inner ring was the three smaller keys and the outer ring was the two large keys.

Byron Easterling was very intrigued when I asked his thoughts on the dream. He shared an insightful interpretation with me, which he later used in a message he spoke. He transcribed my testimony and broke the revelation down into sections in order to glean greater wisdom, knowledge and understanding.

The following is a transcribed version of their interpretations, shared at the "Dreaming With God" conference, held at The Mission.

Byron started by breaking the dream down into parts, creates a diagram of what God was doing.

1st: It came after an impartation, very important.
2nd: Two sets of keys one on a large ring.
3rd: Three more keys on a smaller ring.
4th: There was signet ring of royalty.
5th: Other symbols.

In his message, Byron stated, "I was seeking the Lord for revelation on the meanings. It was from there that patterns began to form from the symbols as each part and symbol brought a divine a release."

He continued, recounting the specifics of the vision: "The keys are of ancient times; he took them and placed them on his left arm. Don't forget- his *left* arm. Why would it be so visual in the dream if it didn't have some importance? The signet ring, possibly a ring of royalty, is it a throw in. Did he just decide to dream about a royal ring that night? I don't think so.

"So, we have these rings. For me the keys represent keys to the Kingdom that operate in your life, [Ramon], or otherwise, gifts and talents God has given you. God has seemingly given you a bit of gifting. It represents that Ephesians passage: 'What if when He ascended that He descended and He took captives and He distributed gifts.' For me, Ramon, the key rings are gifts and talents He has given you. The larger one represents your more prominent gifts- there are a couple of prominent gifts in your life- and three smaller gifts, or lesser gifts, in your life, yet still useful in the Kingdom.

"What really got me about this dream was the left arm, so I went to the Lord and I asked, 'What is this about?' It is really hard to find anything about left arms in the Bible. I kept asking the Lord what this was about, because dreamland is subjective, just like prophecy. That is why we always have to go back and reconfirm [our ideas] with the Lord, and never take anything for granted. Never take a prophecy for granted.

"For me these keys have power. They have anointing. They have blessing, and impartation. When I was talking to the Lord about the left arm, these are the four things He brought up.

"They were releasing:
1. Power.

2. Anointings.

3. Blessings.

4. Impartations, especially.

"Then I discovered this came after an impartation.

"God has something in this impartation. Here is what I think God is saying: you will be able to unite these two rings together. They were joined together. It reminded me of a globe, just like you said, 'rings around a globe.' You are able to use them, not only individually, but you will be able to use them as a group. So you will be able gather them together to increase their potential in the Kingdom.

"It required you putting them on. It came with a *condition* within your dream. So you can't sit back waiting for this, without utilizing your gifts."

Then pausing, he handed the microphone to Phyllis, allowing time for it to sink in.

Phyllis: "The rings with the keys that [Ramon] talked about represented access, but the signet ring spoke of authority. It reminded me of the changing colors changing of the seven Spirits of the churches. The seven Spirits and the different colors that were represented there, and a synergy and a grace, which is interesting as you said that it all started when Carol laid hands on you. And you put the three and the two together, [you get five] the grace for you to walk into these things."

Phyllis then handed the microphone back to Byron.

Byron: "For me, the signet ring was also a sign or seal of authority. [When I got] clarification on the stone or many stones and how the stone/stones laid on the ring, I discovered there was one stone on top of the signet ring. The stones represent authority and they represented authority in your life and as I looked at that, [I realized] they carry varying degrees of strength and beauty and value.

"I asked the Lord, 'What do they mean? What are they all about? The Lord answered: "They are seasons within this authority that are going to come and go. They are going to change, and some will be diamonds, some will be sapphires, some will be amethyst. Each one has a different strength and different beauty and different value, and so within that, you are going to see the changing of the authority in your life and how that is walked out in your life, so, to me, that also applies to grace as well."

"I want to touch on *conditions* on prophecy and dreams. I never really found a prophecy or dream that doesn't have within it conditions, or something that we must do. Why is that? Conditions?"

Pausing, he handed the microphone to Steve.

Steve: "The mention of keys in your dreams, the keys of the Kingdom, Byron, remind us of the text in Matthew 16 where Jesus is talking about keys of the Kingdom. The giving of those keys specifically gives the ability to bind and loose, and it is a binding and loosing that carries in it the safe guard that what you bind and loose has already occurred in Heaven. You are simply giving expression on Earth to what God has already done in Heaven. So those keys, being keys of the Kingdom, are keys that give you the authority, physically, to bind and loose."

"Those words have a great breath to them. We can think of those in context of spiritual warfare or a setting like that. They are talking about the ability to bind and too loose in the spiritual arena. That transcends what we think of normally, in what we think of in spiritual warfare- the ability to release things in other people, the ability to call forth things, the ability to look at things going on in someone's life and say, 'We can bind that because that is something that is detrimental in that person's life.' It is not bringing forth what God has to be brought forth from that life.

"So there are lots of nuances that play out in this business of binding and loosing. But those are keys that have Kingdom authority connected with them. It is the precise nature of those keys. The other thing is to say that binding and loosing is to be directed by the Spirit of God. Through those gifts, through those keys, you can operate with an authority and confidence when those gifts are being exercised, because they are in fact, representation of what Heaven has already appointed. What God has already appointed is now what is being worked out. That is part of that binding and loosing motif that you have, because of the keys of the Kingdom.

"So, just the jumping-off point of the keys being the keys of the Kingdom, is that whole idea of binding and loosing. The other thing that was kind of interesting to me was that stone kept changing. So, you have this changing stone and it replicates, in some respect. Firstly the place you [find] stones is in the layered foundations of the heavenly Jerusalem, pictured in Revelation 21 and 22.

"And there is something else that is interesting about that city: it has a tree in it, the tree of life, which yields a different fruit every month over the course of a year. This is a weird phenomenon. We can't imagine a tree yielding a different fruit every month, but it does. And so, this tree, almost like [the ring], morphs before our eyes as we are witnessing the yielding of a different fruit.

"Well, in a similar way, we are watching the yielding of different stones. Those stones are interesting. They are representations of the apostles. And it all began when Jesus changed Peter's name, Cephas, to Peter in John 1. Cephas is the Aramaic word for 'stone,' and by the time you get to the Book of Revelation, all the apostles are *stones* that are layered into this foundation. Now, the suggestion is that these stones and the tree are somewhat parallel, and that these are different aspects of the way those gifts (the rings and keys) are going to be satisfied. To the needs of the Body of

Christ, the signet ring may, in fact, be the indication of authority that will constantly go through these seasonal shifts, where the gifts that are represented by the keys are concerned.

"So, the really critical thing is that in the dream, for me, was that you had that signet ring, and that the signet ring was an indication of transitioning, ever changing, almost kaleidoscope-like character to the authority. It had a different look in different season. [Your authority] will translate to different looks in different seasons, with a different flavor, a different nuance to it. It may be the same gift, but God changes the *setting* because the season changes. And what is the indication of what the gift is going to be used for? It's regulated by what season it is, and the season will be determined by the nature of the stone.

"What Bryon was saying about the stone makes a great deal of sense. Some stones have a greater quality, a higher value than other stones, at least in the way we value the stones. But each one has its own unique purpose, its own unique hue and color, has its own appointment and design in the purpose of God."

THE POINTS

Listing some strategic points about dreams and prophecy that one should keep as a guide line when receiving revelations.

1. It is important to ask God.

2. Speak and share your experiences with other Charismatic Christians that are knowledgeable about Scriptures.

3. Talk with Christians that use their God-gift's when seeking clarification of revelations in dreams and prophecy.

4. There is always a condition to the revelation; it is not automatic.

5. Search the Word, especially the New Testament. That, in itself, creates growth and a stronger relationship with the Lord on the journey.

I wrote this prayer during one night of release. I would like to pray it with you:

NIGHT "PRAYER OF GRACE"

Father, thank You for this day. Thank You for all the wonderful things You show me. Guide me in all I do, with each and everything You gave me this day, for no day is the same. Each day is an abundance of gifts and mercy from You. Do not let me go through this day or any day without opening and using what You have given me: any and every thing that brings goodness, grace, love, and mercy to You and others around me. Guide me in not judging and putting my opinions into these judgments, for Your wisdom and love is greater than that. What can we do that will bring my brothers and sisters closer to You, so that they may share in You, Lord?

There are times when we all walk away from Your presence and mercy, and don't realize it. So, guide me, and us, Lord, in all we do.

Your love is so enduring and everlasting. Though I spend time with You, I walk, run, and jog with You, I miss You. I want my brothers and sisters to experience what I see and feel more than I do. Your grace, love, and mercy endure forever.

What is there next to do Holy Spirit, my Friend, Companion, Teacher, and my Lord?

Thank You, Father, for Your grace, mercy and love.

Love, Ramon.

Amen.

NIAGARA FALLS

A wise pastor, John Milton, once shared some of the best advice I ever received. He told us (my wife and I) to always chase after each other, like we are first lovers; it is in sharing with one another that we grow closer. It is important to pursue each other in this way, even after the kids are gone. This will keep us growing in our marital relationship.

One time, Lorrie and I took a trip to Niagara Falls, and following Pastor John's advice, we were spending time walking and talking together. On our walk, we watched a little girl with her mother, holding on to the stroller looking over the fence at Niagara Falls. She was asking her mother questions about the waterfalls as we stood together looking at the magnificent rainbows- three distinct arches protruding over the roaring mist. When her mother had finished answering her daughter's questions, I started a conversation with the two of them. Speaking to the little girl I said, "I was taught the rainbow was a message from God, and that He was letting you know He is always close, and always near."

Smiling at them, we turned and began walking away, observing them out of the corner of my eye. The mother smiled. The little girl grabbed her mother's arm, as she had even more questions for her to answer.

We continued our stroll, praying over the people we passed, including a group of monks. Soon twilight was upon us, so quickly we headed back to Toronto. We are the seed of Christ, doing what Christ does: releasing light for flourishing growth. Sometimes, we are a seed or we plant a seed, water them, or plow and till soil. We do this everywhere we go, in everything we do, whether we realize it or not. We can also do the opposite. Beware: we are capable of it. So, choose to love one another and bring life in the words you use.

CHAPTER 6

FEELERS, KNOWERS AND SALVATION

DIFFERENT GIFTS ARE EXPERIENCED by people in unique ways. Sometimes, our gifts manifest in strong feelings or opinions. For example, have you ever come into contact with a person or group and automatically disliked, or virtually hated them, though you couldn't explain why? It could be because of a gift of discernment that communicates to you through your thoughts and feelings. Others receive this kind of information through sight, as in visions and dreams or through direct knowledge that they hear.

Seers can usually see unclean spirits. They may be very blunt in conversation, and give no reason or explanation at the time. Feelers and knowers may not see, but may experience an overwhelming hatred, or other strong emotion, toward a person or group. However, in actuality, they are not really feeling hatred toward the person or group. Their feelings are their discerning reaction toward the principalities, world rulers of darkness and demonic presences attached to the person or group. Their renewed spirit, indwelt by the Holy Spirit, does not like the evil that is present and so reacts toward it with hostility.

Feelers are those who discern different spirits on a person or the surrounding area, in the way their name suggests: through their feelings. They may discern angelic or demonic presences. There are also those whose other senses are attuned to the spiritual realm. Because of this, they may smell or taste what they are discerning. Some smell or taste honey, maple, or gold when angels are present, with the opposite of sulfur, rotting smells or other offensive odors when the demonic or evil critters are around. Knowers know that something is happening around them but they don't know why. They just know. Some call it a gut instinct. Over time and with experience, they can tell you what will happen and it does.

It is the Holy Spirit who releases unknown facts to your knowledge through your sense of discernment, whatever form it takes. He speaks knowledge, including what is going to happen, into the very essence of your spirit. However, many times we do not perceive what He is saying, because our communication link with the Lord is impeded. It can be impeded by many things including being in agreement with lies, drug usage, our actions, the actions of others, or simply having underdeveloped senses, to name a few.

LORRIE

My wife, Lorrie, is both a feeler and a knower.

There were times, before she was even saved, that her gift of knowing showed itself strong. One time, while she was still in her teens, Lorrie's brothers were offered jobs in Palm Springs. They would have to move there to work. When her brothers introduced her to the guy who was promising them jobs, she hated him instantly. Being very blunt and straightforward, she let him know how she felt, without any word of explanation. She didn't care if anyone liked her attitude or not.

Months later, Lorrie found out that the man wanted to use her brothers in a prostitution ring in Palm Springs. She then knew implicitly why she had reacted the way she did. She wondered how many teens and youth had gotten involved with this man.

As you can see from Lorrie's story, there are times that being a well-mannered Christian is not an option. There are times when we must take the Kingdom by force, dispelling the powers of evil that stand in our way. We must protect the innocent, even at the cost of violence. The Lord once spoke to Lorrie about His protective heart for His children, as He draws them into Himself.

These are words Lorrie saw and heard in the Spirit-realm:

I'm seeing a sound go out through the highways and byways,

Out past every dark place.

This sound is light and vibration.

It is breaking all resistance in its path.

Penetrating every hard place.

A warrior's chant of blood.

A victory chant of love.

Yes, a victorious warrior cry of love.

They are being called in.

They do not look like we expect.

I hear Him say, 'CAREFUL Bride.

Careful Bride...'

How you treat Me and Mine."

I hear Him say, "MINE.

Careful how you touch ME and Mine."

SALVATION

In 2007, I had a very busy year as I prepared for two different mission trips, reaching different locations, with different teams in India. The first part of the trip would be one week with The Mission team in Calcutta. We would be traveling to Bicaro for a pastor and leader's conference. The second part would be connecting with Randy Clark and the Global Awakening Team (GA) for ten days in central India. We would be ministering in conferences and a healing crusade.

The spiritual warfare is extreme in many countries where God is not incorporated into its established foundation. Spiritual warfare is like stepping into the boxing ring, a welcome sight for me, from time to time. This is not a comfortable place for many people, as not all are equipped for this. I discovered that my eyes are open in the spiritual dimensions of these countries. For those who have a similar experience, there is breakthrough if one is willing to step out, and partner with the Holy Spirit and angelic intervention that some may know as theurgy.

The Mission team landed in Calcutta, India. We spent the night, then took a five hour train ride to the city of Bicaro. Upon arrival, I noticed that this city in India still had indicators of the Russian military presence that had been established in that city decades ago. We were informed that in this Northern State of India, it is legal to kill a person if they are trying to convert you to Christianity.

We reached a hotel and settled in our rooms. We all got ready for that night's meeting. I was thankful to find that I had been assigned to a room, alone, at the end of the hallway, on the front corner of the building, three floors up; It was my preference to have no roommate if possible.

The leader's conference was being held in a huge tent located on a Methodist's hall grounds, about thirty minutes away from the hotel. The event was hosted by pastors from Calcutta, with whom The Mission leadership had built a relationship over the years.

That first night's event carried a lot of wrestling in the natural and spiritual realm. The equipment was not working properly, people were arriving late and the translators were having problems understanding what we were saying, among other things. The intercessors were facing assaults of different types in the spiritual realm, which kept them buried, not focusing on what was happening. By the end of the night everyone was exhausted from the onslaughts. The team headed back to the hotel to pray into the next day and get a good night's sleep.

WHITE DOVE WITH PEARL WING TIPS

In the night I was suddenly awoken and instantaneously found myself in prayer. I was fully awake, and my prayers went from English to the prayer language (tongues). I had little or no control over the transition of speech from English to tongues, as the Holy Spirit took over.[44] Sometime later, I could pause in prayer, and took a moment to make some hot tea. It was then that I observed myself in my sight for a minute, stepping onto a battlefield covered with armor. Next, I could feel the prayer covering from the people at home in the atmosphere all over me and all around me. Within a couple of hours peace came back into the room and I went to bed.

Early in the morning, just before sunlight broke, I was awakened again. My body felt like it just got out of a fifteen-round, full contact, karate match. I was so glad that the battle in the spiritual realm was over. Or so I thought.

Hearing a commotion outside, I made my way to the window and pulled open the curtain. There I saw three birds outside the window. One bird was hovering in flight in front of the window, just off the ledge. It was a white dove-like bird with glistening pearl wingtips. The other two birds were black and grey and pigeon-like. The white bird had one of the black pigeons in his claws, fighting with it, while the other black pigeon was coming around with a flanking assault to its backside. It was like a scene on a battlefield, when the enemy is trying a surprise attack on the rear flank.

---

44 1 Corinthians 12, 14.

FEELERS, KNOWERS AND SALVATION

This black bird was smart, coming about on a blind side to attack the white bird. Just as the black pigeon was just about to dig its wide open claws into the white bird's back, the white bird shifted its body and whipped his head, striking the black pigeon with its beak directly in its body. It was as though the dove had taken the side of a sword and smacked that black bully with it to show him who's boss. The impact of the beak into the black pigeon body sent it hurling into the air, just as the first rays of sun light breaks through the night sky.

As I was observing the white pearl wingtips of the white bird, the black bird was still flipping through the air backwards from the force of the strike. Once it had regained control of its flight ability, it took off, away from us. The white bird with pearl wingtips turned its full attention to the other black bird in its claws. He gave it a thrashing until he seemed satisfied. Then, in an instant, the white bird with pearl wing tips released its hold, dropping his adversary into the abyss below.

The black bird fell a few feet in the air before it could start flapping its wings; it followed the flight-trail of the other bird. The white bird stood on the window ledge, sun glistening on his pearl wingtips, until both black birds were gone from view, into the far distance. Then he turned his head, looked at me in the eye, gave me what seemed like a nod, it took flight from the window ledge.

I know that what took place that night was in the unseen dimensions manifested as those birds fighting in the natural. The angelic hosts of Heaven stood guard over the team as we slept that night. The black birds were unclean, demonic forces and rulers of darkness that had dominion in this area. They were defeated and let go until it was their appointed time in the abyss.

Remember, each of us has a calling from God, divine in nature that is expressed in both the natural and what is unseen. Our response to it can range from being on a battlefield with prayer covering, to simply encouraging someone at the precise time, to laying on of hands.

The airways were opened. It was just like in a war. And we know, whoever controls the airways controls the battle. You will see more of that in the upcoming story.

SALVATION CALL

As the airways cleared, a freedom opened at the conference, bringing with it supernatural release of Biblical healings, which also opened doors to people's hearts. In my time of ministering to the pastors, leaders and others, I spoke about the needs and desires of one man's heart in telling the story of "A Jacob Heart," which brought havoc, healings, restoration and the breaking of generational curses.[45]

The testimony of Jacob broke open a door, and the men wanted to know more about the Father's heart of love. They asked many questions afterwards. This led to a young coming up at the end of the evening session to speak with me about Jesus Christ. We had an Indian pastor translate our conversation. During our chat, the Lord said, "Ask him if he wants to give his life."

I turned my head, looking at the translating pastor, I repeated those words.

---

45 Previous chapter 2.

"Ask him if he wants to give his life to the Lord." The pastor hesitated. I repeated myself. "Ask him if he wants to give his life to the Lord."

The pastor asked him and he replied, "Yes."

The translator then said, "I will tell the local pastor he came here with. Where is he?"

We couldn't see him.

Fear began to settle in the atmosphere, because of the law legitimizing the murder of any person for converting someone to Christ.

"Have the young man repeat after me," I said. The translator was hesitant because of the laws.

I persisted and the translator finally had the young man repeat the prayer, following the steps outlined in Romans 10:9. We had him ask for forgiveness for his sins, confess that there is only one true God, and ask the Holy Spirit to come and live in him and give him all the truth of Jesus Christ, my Lord and Savior, in Jesus name.

In closing, we asked, "Holy Spirit, come and fill this young man and give him new strength. Amen." When I finished praying, the Indian pastor took the young man to the side and connected him with another pastor that lived in his area.

I walked over to the stage. As I stood there, thanking the Lord for my first salvation to Him, something unusual happened. I lost all strength in my body. I grabbed ahold of the stage to keep from falling flat on my face, but I just did not have strength. But, as I took hold of the stage, I was able to redirect my momentum, swinging into the edge of the platform, hitting it with one knee. I couldn't even keep my eyes open. I had been drained of everything.

I stayed leaning in that position until my strength returned, just before it was time to head back to the hotel. I took someone's arm, needing help to stand after this Kingdom encounter. That night as I left, my heart went out to the young man I had led to the Lord. He was watching me leave. We never got to speak again.

The next day was The Mission team's last day of conferences in Bicaro. At that point, we parted ways when it came time for me to catch the five a.m. train back to Calcutta, for a connecting flight to Hyderabad. I was joining up with the Global Awakening team for the second mission trip.

GLOBAL

When I arrived in Calcutta, I got off the train and made my way to the street where I hailed a taxi with a man getting in the front seat. He asked where I needed to go. I told the driver and asked him the fair amount. The man in the front seat turned, asking for the fair to be paid in to him in advance. I recognized that this was a New York scam, in any language. I told him that I would not pay the drive until we got there. This man kept repeating himself until he finally got out of the cab, a block away.

The driver continued on the way to the domestic air terminal, making it right on time. Having just enough foreign currency, I paid and thanked the driver and the Lord.

More stories of Bidar, India, with Global Awakening and partners India Christian Ministries,[46] can be read in *Chronicles of a Seer*.[48]

---

46 www.indiachristianministries.org.
48 Santos, Ramon. *Chronicles of a Seer*, Chapter 13.

CHAPTER 7

WILLIAM'S STORY, SOUTH AFRICA

HAVING A LIFELONG DREAM of going on a safari became a reality when Toronto Airport Christian Fellowship (TACF) announced that its team, known as Catch the Fire (CTF), was doing an outreach in South Africa that would be followed by a safari tour. Vickie Arnott was leading the CTF trip.[50] The team would head north after arriving in Johannesburg, to spend the first week in Mozambique at Irish Ministries' compound, run by Rowland and Heidi Baker.[51] Upon arrival in Mozambique, the team would begin their outreach by taking an overnight ministry trip, five hours west into, the African bush to minister in rural villages.

The Lord told one member of the team, William, that he could not go out to the villages. He had to stay at the compound and work with the other workers. He really wanted to go, and did not understand the Lord's reasons, but he did what he was told to do. All I could think, in my worldly thoughts was, "He spent

---

50 Santos, Ramon. *Chronicles of a Seer,* Chapter 14.

51 http://www.irisglobal.org/.

thousands of dollars to make this trip, only to spend it working for free? But whom am I to say anything if God told him to?"

William decided he was going to minister to the workers. Unfortunately, he soon found out they had wanted nothing to do with any of the teams that come and go, because of the other ministries that had visited in the past; they said that the people on the ministry teams were all lazy! The workers clearly did not respect them. So William changed his tactic; was going to show them! He worked with the brick makers, making bricks from sun up to sun down, only taking a break when the other workers took breaks. We saw Bill dripping with sweat from head to toe before we left and after we returned.

He never said anything to workers as they tried to work him into the ground, for two and a half days. Finally, one of the brick makers apologized to William, telling him that they tried to break him during the days of work, pushing him well beyond a normal day's work. The worker said to William, "Tell me about your God. I will listen about your God now."

William now had the village workers listening. After they listened, they gave their lives to Jesus Christ, the Son of the One true God. They received the Key of life itself.[52]

William was given a word and he obeyed, using self-control with steadfastness, followed with brotherly affection and love, walking as a personification of Jesus Christ; he was very fruitful.

The teams made it back from the rural villages, with testimonies of healings and miracles. We all had fruit that came from the bush ministry. At first, all we said to William was, "Great!" But, a

---

52 Acts 17:24.

little later, after listening to John Arnott, we realized the importance of the salvations in his story. We realized that "miracles will come and go, but salvation is for eternity" (Luke 10:20). William's work was the cream of the crop, without a doubt.

Thank you William, for listening and doing!

Going on safari was spectacular; if you every get a chance, do it. Being able to share the road with a lion, giraffe, elephant or the other wild animals of that country, where there is no fence, no weapons or guards, feels a little like walking down the street with your pet dog. There is a temptation to reach out of the vehicle and pet the animals. Because of this, there are continual warnings about never sticking any part of your body out the window or vehicle, as you, or that part of you, may never be seen again.

During night safari drives, you can see the animals in the pitch of darkness, when you shine a light on them. Each animal's dietary needs are seen through the color their eyes glow, they say. It is said the differentiating colors lets you know if you may be in trouble, or not. The meat-eaters, or carnivores, have red eyes; the nocturnal omnivores, creatures who sleep during the day and hunt at night and eat everything, have yellow eyes; the herbivores, or plant-eaters have green eyes. I don't know if it is true or not, but I saw all three colors of eyes, all of distinct intensities, during the night drives, and I was not about to put it to the test as we shared the road in the jungle! With the rhinos, all you could see was their black eyes, maybe because most of the animals have three eyelids, or maybe they just wanted to sleep. I would sleep too, if I were them. After all, who is going to bother a herd of rhinoceroses?

SHARING THE ROAD

When you take mission team trips without all the homeland amenities, the teams grow outstandingly in relationship with one another. And in a mixed group, each nationality brings a different flavor to the family. On that trip, our British and Australian mates, Barry and Barrie, always kept us going with their European humor. The Icelanders, a family of professionals, enriched our team greatly. Their son, Thomas, Jr., who had his birthday during the trip, turned fourteen, and received the gift of seeing many released as he lay hands on people, working with the Holy Spirit. At one town, many of the adults prayed for the ill with no results; but when Thomas Jr., laid hands on sick, we saw broken bones mended, eyesight restored, deaf ears opened, to name a few things. Thomas Jr., has begun a legacy because of his parent's openness to step out.

THE CTF TEAM

This team was made up of global members. Ann Marie Sutherland, from Nova Scotia, was like a little sister to me as we talked and picked on one another. We had a historian, Sylvia Dyson, a jewel from the Brazilian Crown of Brazil. I wish I could tell you stories about each of the team members, but that would need to be a book by itself to contain all the adventures we had together.

The last day of the trip was the hardest or at least the most emotional. On trips like this, you bond deeply with those you are with, as you function as a family. I wept as each team member

DEAF EARS OPENED

departed, starting their own journeys home. Waving goodbye to the last face, I boarded my own plane to return home to the USA.

D.C. AIRPORT

When I landed in Washington, D.C., I had some time to kill before catching my connecting flight to San Francisco California. I decided to take a walk and look around at souvenirs in the Presidential shop. There, behind the counter, was a young Arab woman in her mid-to-late twenties. She had an obvious eye problem. The left eye had black lines all around the eye, some very thin, others up to about a quarter inch thick and two to three inches long. And no, it was not makeup. The eyeball itself had black and red lines all through it, even on the pupil. I didn't know if she could see out of her eye, but I thought that if she could, she probably *barely* could.

I continued to scour the store and I found two coffee mugs: one that said "CIA," and another that had the presidential seal in gold. As I got in line to buy the items, I studied her as I prayed under my breath, saying to the Lord, "If You want me to do something, You have to make a way."

Getting to the cash register, I turned around to see a long line of people waiting behind me to purchase the merchandise they selected; there was no time to talk with the cashier. I purchased the mugs and continued to browse around the airport shops until I saw one of my favorite places, Starbucks, and began dreaming of a latté.

While standing in line there, I prayed again under my breath, "Lord, if You want me to do something, you have to make a way!" Then, turning around to see who came up behind me, I saw it was the young Arab woman. We conversed while waiting in line, and I paid for her drink. We continued in conversation as we put condiments in our drinks. When finished, we started walking together and it was then I asked about her eye.

"It happened when I was sixteen," she shared. "I don't remember how. I have been too many doctors and specialists, and have had no reason or explanation for the condition."

I asked if I could pray for her and she answered, "Yes."

We stopped in the middle of the airport corridor. I set my latté on the ground between my feet. Then I placed my right hand over her eye left eye and prayed, "Lord, Thy Kingdom come here on Earth, in her and through her by the power of the Kingdom of God. Please come. I command healing and restoration to her eye in Jesus name. Amen."

It was not the greatest prayer I had ever prayed. I felt dumbfounded. I didn't know what else to do or say.

But, I could feel heat in the palm of my hand, and recognizing this as a sign of God's healing power, I asked her how her eye felt as I starting to take my hand off the eye. I saw no change in what I was seeing until I finished my prayer with, "Thank You, Jesus."

In that instant, all the redness and blackness was gone. Her eye was completely wide open, being completely restored as my hand moved away from her eye.

You could see the surprise on her face, and feel her excitement at being able to see clearly from her eye as she looked around. She asked me for my business card and I handed it to her. I told her that it was Jesus that healed her.

She left, hurrying back to work. A little later, as I walked back by the presidential souvenir shop, I looked in and saw the young lady showing her eye to her friends and telling them with excitement about what had happened. Her female friends were dressed in all-black Muslim attire.

This is the heart of Father's love being released to His children.

It is these types of testimonies that I reach back and grab hold of when life's turmoil rears its head. It doesn't matter what nationality, sex or race you are or what family or community you are from. God loves you.

CATCH THE FIRE TEAM - SOUTH AFRICA

Grant Howard Markus by Joshua

I can neither see nor hear in the spirit like Mariel or Jonathan can. The closest I've come are glimpses of things traveling or standing in the spirit, and the occasional insight to a person's character through their eyes.

I am blessed, and I do seek wisdom despite my failings. Though the enemy may try to steal them, I refuse to let them go or stop seeking wisdom.

I do my best to hide my problems as well as my triumphs. Whether it's reading things I shouldn't, or giving an offering.

I will not lay with a woman until we are married. Since the day my brother got married I have felt the presence of a ring on my ring finger, and it is a reminder that God will lead me to the woman he put on this Earth for me to marry. It has only ever been missing when stolen, and when I pray to God for its return, that whoever stole it, it returns.

I believe that most scientists have stopped trying to find what is hidden to them and refuse to acknowledge the spirit, even though the use of placebos is a form of sorcery. It is, after all, relying on the faith of the patient in the doctor to heal them.

I believe Warlocks and Sorcerers do not comprehend the amount of danger they are in or what blessings are lost to them, when they make deals with spirits.

I believe that there is a thin line between mercy, stopping someone from doing evil, and giving someone a minor punishment for malevolent use of what was, and should have continued to be, a mercy shown.

I believe that an earnest heart and an honest prayer to God will do more good in making a prayer come true, than following a particular protocol. I still think that it's a mistake to just ask God to make a person stop, as it would infringe upon the free will we have all been granted. Because of this, it's unlikely this prayer will be granted. They need to ask for protection, as that does not interfere with free will.

I know that it is the enemy's whispering in the ears of those in power that has led to children being taught what to think, and not how to think, in school. After all, the more a child is taught what to think, the easier it is for his or her values to be molded by those of corrupt ideologies of those in authority.

I believe that God is with me; I'd be dead by now otherwise. The more I see, the more I think about how similar the concept of programming is to genes, physics, the sciences, and what heat level is required to turn a substance from a solid to a liquid and from a liquid to a gas and back again.

CHAPTER 8

GOD HUMOR

FEED THEM AT WORK, REST OR PLAY

HERE IS A PIECE of God's sense of humor in giving us a word in and about everyday life.

I had just gotten back from a morning run, when I went into the backyard while trying to catch my breath. I noticed the foliage had gotten thick on the chardonnay grape vines surrounding the patio, which is not good. What this means is the clusters of fruit would be denied the needed sunlight to sweeten. However, if the clusters got too much sun, it would burn the grapes. If there is not enough sun, disease could set in, especially after a midsummer rain, and it had rained the night before. So, I picked up the pruning shears and my garden pouch as I started pruning back the foliage.

This being one of the times I like to talk with the Lord- while trimming the vines. Pruning away, I heard in my mind, "Foliage is like religion; it has to be pruned so the fruit can receive the light, but it is also part of the fruit's protection." What a paradox, I thought!

While pruning I found a bird's nest with four eggs in it, perched on top of a nice cluster of grapes. I was trimming around the nest, while leaving the nest untouched and the foliage around it thick, to keep the nest hidden. I half asked, half said to the Lord, "Lord, perhaps I will get to see the babies grow as I observe the eggs."

The previous month, as I was doing a pre-flight check on my plane, I found a bird nest in the wheel well with baby chicks in the nest. I moved the nest into a safe area on a broken down plane nearby.

The month before that, I had my business sign taken down at my office because of the company name change. The signage company found a nest with three baby chicks inside the old existing letters. One of my employees, Heather, called her mother and she came and took them home to take care of them, as she mother knew all about birds.

This was a wonderful beginning to summer: going out to prune the grape vines. I grew several varieties including, Sauvignon Blanca, Chardonnay, and table grapes- Ruby Red, Perlette and Thompsons. I loved eating breakfast while pruning the vines. When I reached the rows on the top of the hill, in Muscat and Ruby Red area, I found two more bird nests in the foliage. I stopped for a moment.

"Lord," I asked, "what are You trying to tell me?"

Then, feeling the need to help feed and nurture these baby birds, I went to the pet store and bought a five pound bag of wild bird food and a bird feeder. The smallest bag was five pounds and I figured that was enough food. That way, the mothers of the baby birds wouldn't have to go far for food. I set up the bird feeder at bottom of the rows of vines.

Not long after, I decided to go flying one evening, to log some hours in the airplane. It was one of those long summer days, when it doesn't get dark until about nine o'clock in the evening. Lying in the middle of the taxi lane was a white bag that looked like trash. I taxied around it and went flying. Upon returning much later, parking and tying down the plane, I decided to go get the trash on the taxi way and dump it. As I reached down to pick up the bag, it was very heavy. Being curious about what was in the bag, I carefully opened the bag seeing a brand new twenty pound bag of wild bird feed. Looking up in sky, I said, "Lord, You are funny."

In that moment, I took in the last three month's events with the birds. I asked Lord, "What are You telling me? Is it that I need to feed the birds and You will provide the means?" I began reminiscing about how I always ask for four times the anointing in gifts during prayer. And there it was: four strange events, and four times the bird seed!

"You have shown me three bird's nests, the first with four chicks in it on the plane, the second nest at work with three chicks in it, the third nest at home with two chicks in it."

The revelation was then released. The Lord was speaking loud and clearly in these events to me:

"Feed My children at work, rest or play. What you use or need will be delivered in quadruple."

As I looked to the heavens and said, "Okay Lord, let's do it."

RUBY RED CLUSTERS

STURGIS

It was the middle of summer. Each year, for the last fifty years, motorcycle riders gathered from around the globe in Sturgis, South Dakota for a one-week event that engulfs three weeks or more. The revenue that is brought into the state and its towns during this period carry them through a whole year, fiscally.

Being in the Christian Motorcycle Association (CMA), my chapter was known as "The Lord Knights." There were five of us in the group that decided to go to this year's rally, 1,800 miles away. Kent, on his Police Special, Sean and Jen with the Road King, Larry had the new V-Rod, me, with my Fat Boy FLSTFI, and my son, Jacob, the only non-Harley rider, on a V-Star.

We took I-80 East through Nevada, then cut north through Idaho. Before we left, Sean told his wife that she needed to maintain his strict "no whining" policy, or he would put her on a plane and send her home. I had never seen a woman so quiet.

It was somewhere between Wyoming and Montana, cruising along on single lane highway, that I got a glimpse of the Lord's humor. I love to spend time praying on rides like this, as it is just you and the Lord. Ahead of us we saw two people pulled over to the side of the road. They were running around like chickens with their heads cut off, trying to pick up papers being blown all over the freeway.

We passed them by heading for the next town, and I felt convicted for not stopping to help them; I didn't turn around. I said, "Okay, Lord. I should've stopped and helped. Tell You what, next time I see someone in need, I will pull over and help." The conviction was gone.

Here's a word of warning: When you make a promise, God may show his great sense of humor in helping you fulfill it!

We had just passed through a town when we found that a Highway Patrol officer was slowing freeway traffic down. Let me tell you, I had never seen anything like this before, or ever again since then. When we finally passed by, we saw that there was a hardware truck and trailer pulled over to the side of the road. I looked up towards the sky, nodding my head, smiling. I had made a promise to the Lord. I flipped my bike around on the road, determined to help the truck driver.

Lying in the middle of the road was 4x8 foot sheets of half inch plywood, in both lanes of the highway. The others stopped to see what I was doing, also flipping around. We all helped the driver load the plywood sheets back on his truck.

All this happened just before breakfast. When we stopped at the next restaurant, I told them about the prayer I had said. We continued to stop and help highway travelers who had broken down on the road after that. There is nothing like God-humor as it continued in greater degrees.

Just before Sturgis, I saw two pickup trucks that looked broken down. I felt and saw in the Spirit that something was not right, so I kept on riding. The others chose to stop, and later told me about it. I'm glad I didn't stop; they said that was a drug deal going on! Getting humor and wisdom is a great combination.

LORI

Once, I was standing in a café, listening to Lori, another seer, as she described what she was seeing in the spiritual realm.

First thing in the morning there was a man full of energy, who had not even had his coffee. He said he was just feeling overwhelmed. I know that feeling myself. I had presumed his energy was the adrenaline rush of anticipating his coming caffeine. Listening, I learned a lot more than I had anticipated.

While he was waiting to be handed his coffee at the café, Lori, and a friend, Julie, kept staring at him, through him and around him. In observing her and her friend, I had forgotten she was a seer, until she spoke.

Lori told him, "There is a white robe being put around you, and a hand is over your head." She continued, "I was thinking that it was your guardian angel. But as I watched it, it was not the wing of an angel behind you that you brushed against. And then a wind blew as you manifested what you felt.

"The hand over your head is not an angel as I first thought, because your guardian angel is standing right behind you. The hand I see now and the wisdom from a voice in the spirit tells me that it is the hand of God. The voice said God wants to have fun with you today!" she finished, smiling ear to ear.

This brings me into a greater understanding of what is going on when this happens to me. When I get this surge of joy and energy, it is God wanting to have fun with me!

Seeing what transpired over the man energized him and me more and more as we listened, taking in what was released, taking it with us when we parted company. I, myself, released it into everyone I came in contact with, and it changed their perspectives instantly.

Thank You God for the joy you take in hanging out with me!
Amen.

CHAPTER 9

INDIA AND THE MARK WEST STORY

By Mark West

TO BEGIN, THIS WAS Ramon Santos' first time leading a mission trip going to India. The Lord set up the partnership with India Christian Ministries (ICM) out of Ongole, India. This mission would consist of village ministry, Jesus films, and conferences, concluding with a three-day healing crusade. The team was from North America and included Ramon Santos, Mark West and Wayne Covington from the USA, and David and Beverly Huddleston from Nova Scotia, Canada. We all met and assembled in India for the mission.

THE STEP

In 2007, I, Mark, was attending a conference. Having returned from lunch (at an Indian restaurant), I ran into a friend of mine, Ramon Santos. Ramon was putting a trip together at the end of the year to India and wanted to know if I would consider coming along. I laughed to myself at the coincidence of having chosen to eat at an Indian restaurant for lunch then to be approached, following that lunch, about a trip to India! I asked him to send me the details of the trip once they were available.

I was particularly drawn to this particular India trip. There was group who prophesied over me, saying that I was called to India and would return there, as the Lord had things for me to do there. I knew that this word was true and accurate. The only thing left to work out would be the how and the when of my return came.

The trip was going to cover a two week span from the end of November to the beginning of December. This was a bit of a problem for me because the company I work. So, I needed to find out if my boss would allow me to have time off and if he would be willing to pay me for that extra time.

I arranged a meeting with my boss to discuss the trip and these issues. The good news was that he approved the extra time off and was excited that I had such amazing travel opportunities. The bad news was that he would not agree to pay me for any extra time off, beyond my two weeks of vacation pay. So, I reasoned to myself that I would ask the Lord, not only for finances to cover my trip, but for extra provision to cover my lost wages as well. I was a bit nervous about taking this big step of faith. In the end, however, my curiosity to see what God would do and how He would answer my prayer outweighed any initial hesitation.

I had concern about being away from my son for such a long period of time, as my ex-wife and I shared 50-50 custody of our son. He was four years old at the time, and I was worried about how he would do with me being gone so long. Once again, I had to trust the Lord that, in following His call to India. He would look after my son while I was gone and make sure that the time apart was no more difficult than the times we were apart for only a week. Furthermore, my son's mom was agreeable to the arrangements and was happy to have the extra time with our son while I was gone. All that was left now was to commit to the trip and trust the Lord with the details.

IT BEGINS

The night before my flight to India, I was up several times with a severe case of diarrhea. By morning time, I was feverish and not feeling in any condition to travel anywhere, let alone the twenty plus hours of flying that was ahead. I was extremely miserable once on the flights; I had to battle with and endure whatever symptoms of illness decided to cling to me. I was still burning up with fever, and trying to keep hydrated as I was feeling a bit dehydrated. Thankfully, the flights allowed me time to rest, albeit not in the comforts of my own home.

I arrived in India sometime in the middle of the night, which is typical when flying in to India. I was relieved to see my name on a sign being held by one of the two people who were assigned to pick me up at the airport. After exchanging introductions, Raj informed me that we had two options. My team had already gone on ahead of me to Ongole, which was a six-hour car ride away from where we were in Hyderabad. We could stay the night in a hotel in Hyderabad and then head for Ongole in the morning, or we could journey through the night to Ongole and be in Ongole by morning.

As it turned out, I chose the latter option. In other words, I reasoned to myself, "Why stop now? We have only six more hours to go, so let's get it done so I can be done with the travel portion of this trip and so I can finally be with my team."

It hit me later that I had just asked my two hosts to drive all night. I soon found out, the drive was extremely bumpy and erratic; my plan was to try and sleep the whole ride through.

We pulled into Ongole at about eight thirty the next morning. We were all so happy to reach the end of traveling. My team leader, Ramon, greeted me upon arrival and helped me get checked into my room. After settling in my room, I joined him for breakfast. He briefed me on our schedule for that day, which involved a meeting in a nearby village that evening. This was wonderful news to me, for it meant that I would be able to go back to my room and recuperate. My travels were behind me and I was able to shift my focus to the reason why I had come all this way in the first place. It was time to discover what God had in store for me on this trip and what my role would be in our times of ministry here.

Given all the opposition I had faced on the travel portion, I knew God must have some pretty big things in store for me.

THE TEAM

The first day began as we set out for the first village where we would minister along with showing a Jesus film of the Gospel of Luke in the native language. Wayne Covington taught the ICM team how to set up and use the newly purchased equipment we carried over and would be leaving with ICM for village outreach.

INDIA AND THE MARK WEST STORY

The film was being shown in the heart of this village, which we learned was mainly Muslim and Hindu, with Christians living on the outskirts of the village, being treated as outcasts. The darkness crept in quickly as the area became packed with people. They were drawn in by the sound of worship prior to the film, "The Gospel of Luke," that was played in Telugu, a major language in India. It told the story of Jesus and could be viewed on both sides of the jumbo screen. Many of those from the center of the village could actually watch the film from their homes, from either the windows or back doors, and many came outside to watch the film. This reminded of going to the drive-in theater as a kid.

At the end of the film, we gave a salvation call and about a third of the people stood up, giving their lives to Christ Jesus. Right after this the team moved into healings with the laying on of hands, as the Holy Spirit moved through them. The miracles that flowed showed the power of the blood of Christ. Deaf ears were opened, a broken ankle healed, ligaments that had been torn or damaged were repaired, swellings disappeared, various pains healed, and sight was restored to a person who was going blind. Thank You, Jesus!

Our team was known as Team India. We visited the local pastor's home and child development centers at many locations that were run by ICM. Here, ICM provided the children with a nourishing meal and education each day, as most parents did not always have the means to feed their children each day. The ICM brings

INDIA AND THE MARK WEST STORY

the Father heart of love to the people in fulfilling many of the needs and necessities of life and Team India partnered with them. The team continued in this form of ministry for the next week, moving from village to village until conference and crusade time.

FIRST CONFERENCE

During our first conference I (Ramon) asked any team members who had words of knowledge to come up on the stage and join him. Words of knowledge are revelations given on an individual that the person receiving has no prior awareness of. Mark came up on the stage and joined me with words of knowledge. Mark was handed a microphone. Turning back to view the crowd, I could see a cloud that was moving to my left towards the back of the crowd. I announced, "If you feel anything happening in your body, stand up."

A man who had a tumor the size of a grapefruit on his underarm stood up. He was feeling something. Suddenly, the tumor from his underarm fell off to the ground! The skin of his underarm, where the tumor fell off, was pink and white, and was healing so completely that it had returned his natural brown color. We heard this report of healing in a manner of minutes, from those standing next to him.

Mark gave the words of knowledge that he was receiving, asking those people in the crowd who had the symptoms that he called out to stand. He called out, "Jesus wants to heal you! Standing up is an act of belief!" As they were standing, Jesus healed those with infirmities as Mark gave thanks to Jesus. There were hundreds of healings that day as we cursed aliments, injuries, and cancers. The man healed from the tumor, brought the tumor to the front of the stage and left it on the ground at the end of the night before leaving. We thanked the Lord for allowing us to make a difference in that person's life.

How can a person say, "There is no Jesus," or "There is no God," to a person who has just been healed, or to the person is who watching the healing take place? How did we see so many miracles? You see, we didn't believe the lie that Jesus doesn't do miracles, signs, and wonders anymore; those days of old are over. We went after the knowledge that has been withheld by some:

> *You're hopeless, you religion scholars! You took the key of knowledge, but instead of unlocking doors, you locked them. You won't go in yourself, and won't let anyone else in either (Luke 11:52, MSG).*

We said to the crowd, "Always give thanks to God, no matter how small the healing." The word spread and the crusade grew

INDIA AND THE MARK WEST STORY

those three nights. There were about 1,500 people that came the last night to see and learn about Jesus and who He is today, tomorrow and was yesterday.

Here, in the picture above, Team India is partnering with ICM in blanket distribution for those in need. This is also a necessity for rural villages. The finances donated by those who wanted to be a part of Team India's outreach, was used for this purpose. These funds were also used for food distribution. Some cash funds were given to ministries, as you could see those ministers who spent all they had on their congregation and others, whether Christians or not, to show the love of the Father by giving whatever was needed.

David and Beverly are such a gracious couple, and incredible to minister with. Beverly, a retired schoolteacher, helped and taught me about ministering to children. David, a retired Canadian Fighter Pilot Commander, has great tactics in foreign affairs and in ministry. We learned much from each other in the places we went traveling together.

TEAM INDIA

CLOSING

When life's challenges give you a chance to become better and do better, remember these words that were given to me, spoken by Theodore Roosevelt, the twenty-sixth president of the United States of America:

> *"It is not the critic who counts, not the man who points out how the strong man stumbles, or where the doer of deeds could have done better. The credit belongs to the man in the arena, whose face is marred by dust and sweat and blood, who strives valiantly...who knows the great enthusiasm, the great devotions; who spends himself in a worthy cause; who at the best knows in the end the triumph of high achievement, and who at the worst, if he fails, at least fails while daring greatly, so that his place shall never be with those cold and timid souls who have never known victory nor defeat."*[53]

---

53 April 23,1910, Sorbonne, Paris speech, "Citizenship in a Republic."

OTHER QUOTES BY TEDDY ROOSEVELT

"Believe you can and you're halfway there."

"It is hard to fail, but it is worse never to have tried to succeed."

"The only man who never makes mistakes is the man who never does anything."

This is the beginning of the challenge:
Will you continue the journey with me and others?
The necessities and needs of life are in each of us, both in the natural and the supernatural. Whether you are a seer, hearer or even if you believe you have no giftings, there will always be needs or necessities within each of us that release the giftings, if only you will be willing to take a step forward.

The Truth is out there. It brings freedom, life, power and love. Don't miss out on True Love, in all forms, by having walls up, or by hardening your heart or mind, thinking that you're protecting yourself from pain. It is good to always protect your heart, but you must step out or you will miss out. We will all get hurt sometimes.

There are not always scientific facts to answer all of our questions, or tie up every loose end at this moment in time. But Truth is real. Take a risk; step out, or miss out.

—*Ramon*

APPENDIX

Goll, Jim. *The Seer.*, Destiny Image Publishers, Inc. 2004, www.destinyimage.com.

New Exhaustive Strong's Numbers and Concordance with Expanded Greek-Hebrew Dictionary. Copyright © 1994, 2003, 2006, Biblesoft, Inc. and International Bible Translators, Inc. www.biblesoft.com.

For more information about the ministries mentioned in this book, I highly recommend their websites.

www.Globalawakening.com

http://www.dewnamis.com

www.GODsGenerals.org

www.williambranham.com

Randy McKenzie: www.explorationfilms.com

TACF: www.TACF.org

Byron Easterling: www.bhhinc.org

Steve Carpenter: www.christianfellowshipministry.org

Phyllis Miller: The Dream Team: www.destined2dream.com

MIST

Genesis 2:5-6: "*When no bush of the field was yet in the land and no small plant of the field had yet sprung up—for the Lord God had not caused it to rain on the land, and there was no man to work the ground, and a mist was going up from the land and was watering the whole face of the ground."*

Job 36:27-28: *"For he draws up the drops of water; they distill his mist in rain, 28 which the skies pour down and drop on mankind abundantly."*

Psalm 148:7-8: *"Praise the Lord from the earth, you great sea creatures and all deeps, fire and hail, snow and mist, stormy wind fulfilling his word!"*

Jeremiah 10:13: *"When he utters his voice, there is a tumult of waters in the heavens, and he makes the mist rise from the ends of the earth."* (This speaks of rising one up.) Mist: (speaking of a leader, prince, governor). Rise: (root; to ascend, intransitively (be high) or arise (up), ascend up.

Hosea 13:3: *"Therefore they shall be like the morning mist or like the dew that goes early away, like the chaff that swirls from the threshing floor or like smoke from a window."*

James 4:14: *"Yet you do not know what tomorrow will bring. What is your life? For you are a mist that appears for a little time and then vanishes."* (An atom in time.)

FOAM

Psalm 46:1-4: *"God is our refuge and strength, a very present help in trouble. Therefore we will not fear though the earth gives way, though the mountains be moved into the heart of the sea, though its waters roar and foam, though the mountains tremble at its swelling. Selah."*

Jude 1:12-13: *"These are hidden reefs at your love feasts, as they feast with you without fear, shepherds feeding themselves; waterless clouds, swept along by winds; fruitless trees in late autumn, twice dead, uprooted; wild waves of the sea, casting up the foam of their own shame; wandering stars, for whom the gloom of utter darkness has been reserved forever. It was also about these that Enoch, the seventh from Adam, prophesied, saying, 'Behold, the Lord comes with ten thousands of his holy ones.'"*

ABOUT THE AUTHOR

RAMON SANTOS has been hearing from God since he was a young child. His life has been marked by strange and unusual events that point to the fact that God has continuously intervened and directed his life. From divine appointments, direct dialog with God, and avoiding close calls, to delivering accurate prophetic words, participating in deliverance, and being actively involved in the charismatic movement, Ramon Santos has devoted his gift as a seer, his ability to see into the spiritual realm, to the advancement of God's Kingdom on the earth. Ramon a former US Marine or should as he puts it still a Marine only released from active service.

A businessman and licensed as a minister with The River in Northern California, he is also a part of Global Legacy. Ramon, having led numerous teams on short-term mission to India, also has a history of working with home churches and other ministries. He has a second ministry license with Global Awakening upon going to Pennsylvania to receive his anointed covering under Randy Clark. Ramon, and his wife Lorrie, are active members of The Mission Church in Vacaville, California where they live.

OTHER BOOKS BY RAMON SANTOS

Chronicles of a Seer

Available for sale on Amazon.com

Made in the USA
San Bernardino, CA
11 March 2014